TEACHING SCIENCE

Edited by

JENNY FROST

Institute of Education
University of London

Photographs by
RICHARD INGLE
JENNY FROST

THE WOBURN PRESS

First published in 1995 in Great Britain by
THE WOBURN PRESS
Newbury House, 900 Eastern Avenue
London IG2 7HH, England

and in the United States of America by
THE WOBURN PRESS
ISBS, 5804 N.E. Hassalo Street, Portland, OR 97213-3644

British Library Cataloguing in Publication Data

Teaching Science. – (Woburn Education
Series)
  I. Frost, Jenny   II. Series
507

ISBN 0–7130–0185–2 (cased)
ISBN 0–7130–4015–7 (paperback)

Library of Congress Cataloging-in-Publication Data

Teaching science / edited by Jenny Frost.
    p.cm.—(Woburn education series)
  Includes bibliographical references and index.
  ISBN 0–7130–0185–2.—ISBN 0–7130–4015–7 (pbk.)
    1. Science—Study and teaching (Elementary)—Great Britain.
  2. Science—Study and teaching (Secondary)—Great Britain.
  I. Frost, Jenny.
  LB1585.5.G7T45   1995
507′.1′241—dc20   93–48381
                                      CIP

Printed in Great Britain by
Bookcraft (Bath) Ltd, Midsomer Norton, Avon

TEACHING
SCIENCE

THE WOBURN EDUCATION SERIES
General Series Editor: Professor Peter Gordon

CONTENTS

ACKNOWLEDGEMENTS

I should like to thank Peter Gordon for his invitation to write the book and for his help and guidance during its preparation; Alastair Cuthbertson for reading an earlier draft and providing valuable criticism; Paul Pilkington for preparing the format of the book on the computer and undertaking much of the initial typing; Janet Maxwell for preparing the diagrams; and Harry Frost for help in checking the script.

I am indebted to the headteachers and students of the schools listed below, for permission to take photographs and to the teachers who appear in the photographs, namely: Chris Askwith, Roshani Croos, Christine Fuggle, Neil Jordan, Patrick King, Paul Mostyn, Samantha Perkins, Adrian Simms, Urmala Tiwari, Sheila Turner, Mike Vingo, Cornelia Williams, Steven Williams, Brenda Wood; as well as to a number of teachers who allowed us to photograph their lessons, even though the photographs do not appear in the final selection.

Particular thanks must go to Richard Ingle who not only took more than half the photographs, but undertook the labour of labelling carefully films and prints, with great accuracy, so that we could locate the negatives as necessary at a later date.

I should also like to thank the following for permission to reproduce material: Department for Education; John Murray Publishers; County of Avon Primary Science Working Party, 1984; Longmans Publishing; School of Education in the University of Durham.

Schools where photographs were taken:
Archbishop Michael Ramsey School, London Borough of Southwark;
Cavendish School, Hemel Hempstead, Hertfordshire;
Trinity School, Esher, Surrey;
Raynes Park Boys School, London Borough of Merton;
Riddlesdown High School, London Borough of Croydon;
Richmond Tertiary College, London Borough of Richmond;
Sir William Collins School, London Borough of Camden;
Walsingham Girls School, London Borough of Lewisham.

NOTES ON CONTRIBUTORS

The writers are senior lecturers or lecturers in the Science Education Department at the Institute of Education, University of London, which is responsible for pre- and in-service professional development courses for science teachers for both primary and secondary schools, as well as for advanced studies and research in science education. The department has up to 90 beginning science teachers each year on the Post Graduate Certificate of Education course.

Jenny Frost taught in West Africa and in a London Comprehensive School before joining the Institute of Education in 1970. Professional interests cover both primary and secondary science. She has undertaken research on the implementation of balanced science courses in secondary schools and is currently researching the application of statements of competence to the professional development of science teachers. She has undertaken consultancies both in the UK and abroad. Her writing includes titles in the *Nuffield 13–16 Series,* chapters in *Science in the Locality* (1985), and consultancy for the Primary science series *Let's Explore (1992).*

Leslie Beckett taught in West African and London comprehensive schools before working in Malaysia as a science adviser. He later joined the ILEA advisory team before coming to the Institute in 1982 . He has a strong interest in distance learning and has prepared materials for the Open University, India and Nairobi. His writings include contributions to the *APPIL* Independent learning project, and *Maintaining Choice in the Secondary Curriculum* (1981), published by the Council for Educational Technology.

Arthur Jennings taught biology in Hertfordshire schools before joining the Institute. He has extensive experience in science teacher education and has made contributions to several international conferences. His research interests include assessment in science and the application of statements of competence to professional development. His writings include *Science in Schools, Which way Now?* (1978); *Science in the Locality* (1985) and *National Curriculum Science – so near and yet so far* (1992).

Sheila Turner held a variety of posts before coming to the Institute in 1978; these included teaching science and biology in schools and working as a home tutor. Professional interests cover both primary and secondary science teaching. She has undertaken consultancies in several countries including Indonesia, India, Kenya and China. Her research has focused on nutrition education; she led a research project for the Health Education Authority on catering for healthy eating in schools. She was a member of the ASE Multicultural Education Working Party and has chaired the Education Division of the Institute of Biology. Her writing includes materials for teaching science, e.g. *Nutrition Workshop,* as well as contributions to *Race, Equality and Science Teaching.*

Tony Turner taught science in schools before taking up a curriculum development post in the West Indies. He was a Nuffield research fellow for two years before joining the Institute in 1976. His research interests include the science, mathematics interface, and issues of culture and race in science. He has undertaken consultancies in China, Russia, Pakistan and Africa. His writings include contributions to *Race, Equality and Science Teaching* (ASE, 1992). He is currently involved in the development of school-based teacher education.

LIST OF PLATES

4   Scientific Investigations and Technological Tasks

Lesson 1 Planning an investigation

Lesson 2 Putting an experimental plan into action

Lesson 3a 'Brainstorming', the start of the technological task

5   Circus

Circus on interference of waves

6   Independent Learning

Note about the photographs

The photographs were taken in a variety of schools in and around London by Richard Ingle and Jenny Frost. In the final selection an attempt was made to reflect the many different ethnic groups in our schools and to give equal space to men and women, boys and girls. Some of the photographs, such as those of the circus lesson in Chapter 5, however, were taken in single-sex schools, of which there are still several in London. The photographs of the practical skills lesson were taken in a mixed school with a much higher proportion of boys than girls. (This imbalance is caused by the presence of an all-girls school in the locality.)

LIST OF FIGURES

PREFACE

Jon Ogborn

This very welcome book is packed with practical ideas and advice for the beginning science teacher. It is based on three simple principles regarding teaching methods: a principle of variety; a principle of careful and appropriate choice; and a principle of skilful and carefully prepared implementation. Through a wide range of examples, the authors discuss in richly illustrated detail what these principles involve in practice. All the examples are real ones taken from recent classroom experience, made more vivid by a large collection of photographs documenting the steps and phases involved in each kind of approach.

There are some who accuse University teacher-trainers of purveying what they are pleased to call 'trendy theory'. This book flatly gives the lie to any such idea. There is, in the best possible sense, nothing 'trendy' about it at all. The ideas discussed are well tested, and the advice given is based on extensive experience in a wide variety of schools and circumstances. The book is, however, also thoroughly up to date, discussing needs which arise out of recent changes in the science curriculum, and how science teachers can creatively respond to them. Its messages are timeless, but also timely.

Although primarily a book for the beginner, there is much in it to commend to the more experienced teacher. As time goes by we all tend to get a little settled in our ways, doing again what has worked well in the past. This book may help remind the experienced teacher of methods and strategies which can refresh the parts of the curriculum that other methods can not reach. And just by suggesting a change of style from time to time, it may help to rekindle enthusiasm and interest.

The book will also be essential reading for teachers in schools who accept the responsibility of mentoring beginning teachers. The particular school in which the beginning teacher happens to begin to practise the craft of teaching cannot be a paradigm for all schools; it simply provides one particular concrete context in which to learn. Thus the mentor needs to be aware, not only of the well-practised methods which can be seen and assimilated in that school, but of a larger and more varied set of approaches which the beginning teacher needs to start to build into her or his repertoire.

A craft such as teaching, like a craft such as pottery, cannot be learned from a book. Doing it is of the essence. But a book does have something to contribute. Like Bernard Leach's classic *A Potter's Book*, this book is full of that practical, concrete and specific advice which helps to get the beginner started, which points to where things may have gone wrong and so to how to do better another time, and which reminds experienced teachers of knowledge and skill they have forgotten they possess so that they can pass it on to beginners through talk as well as by example.

1
INTRODUCTION
Jenny Frost

Learning to teach

This book about the teaching of science in secondary schools is written mainly for beginning teachers[1] and for the teacher trainers who work with them. The latter group will include not only people like the authors, who are tutors in a university department of education and who work with and supervise beginning science teachers, but the increasing number of science teachers who will carry a wider responsibility for teacher training[2] than hitherto.[3]

When training for any profession, beginners start with a tentative picture in their minds of what the work entails and the skills that will have to be learned. The pictures of teaching brought to the start of training are probably more vivid than for most other professions, because everyone spends about eleven years of their formative years on the 'other side' of teaching; that is, eleven years of 'teacher watching'. The dominant memory for most people is of the teacher at the front talking to the whole class. Even where teachers spent only a small proportion of their time on this, it is still the image least likely to fade. Memories of what teachers might have been doing while classes were busy on practical work, or engaged in writing or discussion are hazier, and there are virtually no ideas of what was involved in lesson preparation merely because this was not seen. Teaching science, like teaching any subject, does, however, require a wide range of professional skills and knowledge; standing at the front talking to the whole class is only one of the many skills that beginning teachers have to learn. Part of becoming a teacher must therefore involve developing a greater awareness and understanding of the tasks that teachers undertake both during lessons and in preparation beforehand than can be gained simply by relying on memory of one's own teachers.

Teacher watching can also be misleading in another way, especially if the teacher is good. Good teachers appear to perform effortlessly; they have resources ready to hand; questions that intrigue and challenge their classes come readily to their minds; they select appropriate explanations, analogies and metaphors for almost any situation that arises; their timing and organisation are flawless; they respond to the needs of the class and of individuals; the environment in which they work is stimulating. Their ease of performance masks the knowledge they have and the complexity of the task:

> Teachers have knowledge which enables them to undertake complex tasks in the day-to-day events of their professional lives. Much of this knowledge drives routines which are put into action in an almost unthinking way and teachers are unable to explain what they have done during a lesson or why they have done it. Teachers obviously have a

great amount of tacit or intuitive knowledge which influences what they and their students do in classrooms. (Tobin, Butler Kahle, Fraser, 1990, p.35)

Anyone who has been in teacher training will be able to give examples of how an analysis of a lesson surprised the teacher concerned. For instance, one of the writers of this book, working with a group of beginning teachers in a school, had asked the group to record everything a particular teacher did in the first few minutes of a lesson. The laboratory had movable tables in the centre and fixed benches round the edge. The teacher moved the tables rapidly to form a circle, asking the class to wait quietly outside. As the class came in members took their places at the tables, which placed them and the teacher automatically in an appropriate position for a class discussion which occupied the first twenty minutes of the lesson. The reorganisation of the room and moving the class in had taken less than three minutes. When the teacher listened to the analysis of his actions afterwards he commented: 'That's interesting, I never noticed I was doing it ... but yes you're right, it was important.'

For the purposes of this book we have focused on one area of science teachers' expertise, namely the ability not only to use a range of teaching strategies but to be flexible in the use of the strategies, changing from one to the other as the situation requires. Ability depends partly on having a picture of what these strategies might be and the tasks associated with each. We have selected different types of lessons to illustrate a considerable repertoire of the strategies that would be part of the routine 'stock-in-trade' of an effective science teacher. The organisation and management of time, spaces and resources associated with the strategies, the relevant planning and the reasons for using the strategies are all explored. General points are supported by examples of specific lessons or series of lessons, some of which are illustrated with photographs.

The selection shows teachers frequently undertaking some task other than standing at the front and talking to the whole class and may help to address the question often asked by beginning teachers: 'What do I do if the students are getting on by themselves?'

The descriptions may seem obvious, even trivial at times, especially to experienced science teachers, but they are none the less essential for a beginner, just as the descriptions of how to start a car and put it into gear, obvious and apparently intuitive to the experienced driver, are essential to the learner driver.

The organisation of the book

The chapters can be read as self-contained units, although it would pay to read Chapters 1 and 2 before any of the others. There is inevitably some repetition, but this does not matter because it is useful for beginning teachers to find that skills learned in one context are applicable in another.

The descriptions start in Chapter 2, 'Teaching skills'. Arthur Jennings takes the reader on a tour of science lessons showing snapshots of the varied work of a science teacher; asking questions; demonstrating; giving an exposition; arranging for students to watch a videotape; listening to students reporting investigations; marking students' work; and considers the possible purpose a teacher might have for selecting each strategy. Arthur Jennings asks the reader to keep in mind two questions: first, 'What is the teacher's intention and how is the intended learning encouraged?' and second, 'What demand is being made on the students and what learning is occurring?'.

Chapter 3 identifies the scope and limitations of four different types of practical work. It considers the teacher's role not only in the management of up to thirty students engaged in practical laboratory activities, but also in making the experience meaningful, in order to avoid practical work becoming no more than recipe following. The chapter shows safety considerations, the need for the 'prepared mind' on the part of the student and the need for allowing enough time to talk through the significance of any practical experience. The three lessons photographed all lasted approximately fifty minutes: the ability to use a range of teaching strategies within that relatively short space of time is abundantly clear, particularly in the lesson on fire fighting.

Chapter 4 on scientific investigations and technological tasks continues the theme of practical work. Their justification is given not so much in terms of their simulating what scientists and technologists do but in terms of their providing yet another situation in which students can take responsibility for their own learning. The phases of the investigations and tasks are described along with the roles of students and teachers during each phase. This chapter is the only one which contains photographs from a series of lessons (three lessons on a technological task) and hence has more photographs than any other chapter. The sequence is important because it shows how a teacher broke a task into sections that had some coherence in themselves and fitted the time slots, and yet provided continuity between one lesson and the next. Mention is also made of the need for explicit teaching necessary for students to learn how to investigate. Of particular significance is the potential for a teacher to develop learning related to the nature of science and the nature of evidence.

Tony Turner's Chapter 5 on 'The Circus' provides a bridge between the chapters on practical work and on independent learning. A 'circus' is a series of activities focused upon one particular theme, and this is illustrated by his varied examples. Students move from activity to activity without continual reference to the teacher. The activities are not necessarily practical in the traditional sense but must engage the student in active learning. A circus often lasts for about an hour but may spread over three or four double lessons, and hence it is rather like short-term independent learning. It calls for particular management skills. The roles a teacher plays in initiating and introducing a circus, in helping while the circus is in progress and in drawing ideas together at the end are similar to those required for more full-scale independent learning.

Leslie Beckett in Chapter 6 then explores the potential and management of independent learning in greater detail. He highlights the need for the appropriate collection, preparation, labelling, storage and maintenance of resources, especially book resources, if this method of learning is to be successful. He reiterates Tony Turner's points about the need for clear written instructions and the ability on the part of the teacher to know when and how to intervene. Many of the skills of the teacher described in the snapshots of separate lessons in Chapter 2 are still part of the armoury of a teacher operating an independent learning scheme. The teacher on occasions gives an exposition to the whole class, demonstrates, marks books. The chapter is illustrated by examples drawn from the lower, middle and senior parts of secondary school.

Sheila Turner's Chapter 7 on games and simulations starts with a classroom debate on fluoridation of water. This chapter provides examples of children actively playing with abstract ideas removed from the 'distracting clutter of reality' often produced by practical work:

> Science deals with theoretical concepts and their interrelationships. They are abstract and manipulated in the abstract. It is essential that these concepts are separated from their concrete reality if the maturing scientific mind is to gain mastery over them. (Woolnough and Allsop, 1985, p.39)

Sheila Turner shows how games and simulations (including computer-based ones) can allow students to manipulate and confront abstract ideas in an educationally stimulating and enjoyable context. We see parallels to the example of a circus where students manipulate models of isomers. In all her examples she highlights the preparation needed beforehand, questions of classroom management, the briefing and debriefing required and how to fit these activities into a longer learning sequence.

Discussion forms an important strategy in all contexts. In Chapter 8 Arthur Jennings considers ways in which it can be used by teachers. He emphasises the importance of a classroom climate where students are prepared to listen to each other and entertain each other's ideas. In his six examples of small group discussions the need for adequate preparation of the participants' prior knowledge of the subject under discussion is apparent, showing that discussion is not a 'one-off' activity but part of a sequence of learning. The summary phase of the class discussion reveals the possibility for drawing out three different messages, similar to the varied learning that can be drawn from a problem solving exercise.

Beginning teachers who trained at the London Institute of Education will see a similarity between the structure of this book and a session run at the start of the PGCE course (Post Graduate Certificate in Education). The main objective of the session is to provide a way for beginning teachers to confront their own beliefs about teaching and learning. The 80 or so beginning teachers are divided into classes and attend a series of science 'lessons', given by different tutors. Each tutor uses a different teaching strategy. Beginning teachers move from 'lesson' to 'lesson' at specified times like students in school. Photographs of these lessons were taken and used to produce descriptions, in poster form, of what each teacher was doing at different phases of the lesson. The photographs often illustrated the *introduction*, *activity* and *summary* phases but it was possible to infer what had gone on at the *planning* stage and what might be suitable *consolidation* or follow-up. This was repeated for several years and each year the descriptions of a particular type of lesson revealed similarities with those from previous years. To some extent this stability can be attributed to the limited turnover of staff in that period, the fact that the same person produced the posters and that a group of people teaching together subconsciously grow like each other. But some changes in staff and a different person taking the photographs did not significantly alter the situation. These analyses, which were made of tutors teaching adult graduates, have been mirrored in our observations of teachers in schools; hence the origin of the book.

Understanding the learner's perspective

Understanding the learner's perspective is of course important for teaching and plays a significant part in professional training. Reflecting on one's own experience as a learner, learning from the experience of observing students in school and reading about learning provide the knowledge base for this understanding. Important amongst the reading is the extensive literature on the 'constructivist' approach to teaching and learning in science, which views learners as active constructors of their own knowledge.

Much of the research in this area focused initially on what were the existing ideas which students brought ready-made to science lessons and these are now well documented. Early research in the 1960s and 1970s charted physics concepts for the secondary age range, but was later extended into chemistry, biology and astronomy and the age range increased to include primary children and adults (Osborne and Freyberg, 1985; Driver, 1985). In some ways this can be seen as an extension of the work done by Piaget who studied, among other things, children's ability to make sense of physical phenomena. He found, for instance, that when the same volume of water is poured into a wide container and a tall thin one, children often perceive the tall thin one to have more water in it than the short wide container. Many children would predict that if a heavy object, like a lump of lead, is put into a jar of water it will displace more water than a lighter object of the same volume, say a lump of aluminium. Demonstrations that the rise in the water was the same in both cases often failed to convince.

Many of the ideas which are held are in conflict with scientific ideas, which makes the task for the science teacher more interesting. Examples of ideas which conflict with scientific ideas are that gravity becomes significantly stronger the further away from the earth; that the bubbles which come out of boiling water are made up of hydrogen and oxygen; that light travels further at night than during the day; that plants obtain food ready-made from the soil. There are instances quoted of where students appear to know the accepted science, for instance that the world is round, but where their conceptualisations of this are very different from the teacher's (Nussbaum, 1985). Some of the research has focused on how students use words. For most young people, for instance, 'animal' does not include people, and 'plant' does not include trees.

In most cases it is not difficult to understand how the ideas have developed. They may have considerable explanatory power (gravity must be stronger higher up because if you drop from a higher point you hit the ground harder). They may be close to perceptions as in the case of the water and the flasks from Piaget's work. They may be embedded in everyday language and images such as notices which read 'no animals allowed in the shop' and the fact that 'trees' (and 'weeds' for that matter) are distinguished from 'plants' in the ordinary gardening sense.

Similar findings occur in different countries; they do not appear on the whole to be culturally dependent. They have been found in adults, both with and without a formal science background. People with a formal science training have been found to use scientific ideas in response to problems set in a science context (laboratories/tasks set on science courses) but to use conflicting mental models in everyday situations. The tenacity of the models has itself been intriguing; there are many instances of 'explaining away' discrepancies such as a child who claimed that the water used for the Piaget displacement experiments must be 'magic', and instances where the old models return to replace scientific models learned at the time quite successfully in science lessons (Gauld, 1989). Parallels have been drawn between this and scientists who hold on to existing theories despite conflicting evidence, as, for instance, Cavendish with his belief in caloric theory.

Such research has helped many teachers to have greater insight into learners' problems and an understanding that while students may have the 'wrong' scientific idea they may nevertheless be thinking and reasoning scientifically, that is, holding ideas which are consistent with some evidence. Many writers in this field, reflecting on the way learners make sense of their science, have viewed the learner as a scientist trying to make sense of new ideas and events. One of the better known is Ros Driver's book (1983), which has the metaphor of the *Pupil as Scientist* as its title.

While greater sensitivity towards a learner and greater understanding of thought processes are undoubtedly valuable to a teacher, the question remains as to the extent to which teachers can build deliberately on this research in the way they teach. There is a growing literature on teaching approaches which have been built on this knowledge of children's ideas. These approaches are based on the notion that 'cognitive dissonance' is necessary for learning; that is, that people learn when they find their ideas somehow do not make sense and find the need to resolve the conflict. They are also based on the belief that just as people construct their original ideas for themselves using existing experience they must construct new ideas for themselves using experiences which the teacher makes available to them. The role of the teacher is to elicit students' initial thinking, to find some way of challenging it, thus providing the necessary cognitive dissonance. The next step is to provide explanations which will resolve the dissonance, requiring students to use the new explanation themselves. The further reading at the end of the chapter gives accounts of such a teaching approach.

While there is no lesson described which follows the approach rigidly, many lessons have echoes of it. The lessons do, however, all have examples of active learning because:

The good thing in much of what has been identified as 'good practice' is its commitment to active rather than passive learning. We share that commitment to a form of science education in which children learn science by doing things, doing them both in the hand and in the head. (Driver and Millar, 1987, p. 56)

Understanding the learner's perspective can also be enhanced by the research into the role of language in learning. The use of discussion and writing, not just as a means of communication but as a means of formulating ideas, is apparent in many lessons. Chapter 8 covers the background to this.

Commentary

As well as the main theme of teaching strategies there are other themes which recur throughout the book: the need for teachers to have clear objectives while not working to a tight objectives model; the need for a teacher to be a good listener; that diagnostic teaching is essential as teachers take a greater role in assessment; that students must be given the opportunity to manipulate ideas; that learning is a social activity involving interaction both among students and between students and teacher.

The authors are aware that the teaching strategies described are dependent on good classroom discipline and involve considerable commitment in terms of time, particularly in preparation. The need for good technical support for science is also evident. Resource management is notoriously understaffed and yet it is a key to success in most of the strategies used.

In compiling this book there is no attempt to reduce the essential human interaction between teachers and their classes to a set of rules. Human passion, commitment to learning, respect for science and respect for individuals defy such constraints. F. W. Westaway, writing about science teaching in 1929, wrote 'the last thing we desire to find in a teacher is that he has surrendered his own individuality and teaches in accordance with someone else's hard and fast rules'. Joan Solomon wrote in 1980 that 'to lay down some new techniques of teaching...could do violence to the personal variations which are inherent in teaching' (Solomon, 1980). Learning to teach involves 'a new way of being yourself' (Black, 1987), not copying someone else's actions; hence another reason for the preference for the phrase 'teacher education' rather than 'teacher training'.

Other books on teaching science

Sharing and discussing the processes of teaching are important in professional development. The long descriptions of 'If I were teaching this I would explain it thus...' of the original *Nuffield Physics Teachers Guides* (1965) were of immense value to me as a young teacher, although frustratingly long and unnecessarily avuncular in style for many experienced teachers. *A Guide to Classroom Observation* (Walker and Adelman, 1975), *Classroom Teaching Skills* (Wragg, 1984), *Teaching Children in the Laboratory* (Solomon, 1980), *Learning in Science: The Implications of Children's Science* (Osborne and Freyberg, 1985) and *Active Teaching and Learning Approaches in Science* (Centre for Science Education, Sheffield, 1992) are other examples of ways in which writers have shared ideas about teaching with others. The 'further reading' at the end of this introduction provides a selection of books or parts of books from the increasing literature on classroom practice which have proved useful to science teachers; not only to beginning and experienced teachers wanting to develop their range of teaching strategies, but to people taking on teacher education either as a tutor or as a teacher responsible for beginning teachers in school.

There remain only a few further comments. First the book does not cover directly questions of content, although examples have been selected from all branches of school science. Second, we debated whether to refer to learners in schools as 'pupils' or 'students'. We eventually decided on the latter, partly because it is becoming fairly widely used and partly because it indicates that learning is as much the responsibility of the learner as of the teacher. Third, we had to decide how closely to tie the book to the national curriculum in science in the UK. On the whole we have avoided this so that the labels 'attainment targets', 'statements of attainment', 'levels of attainment' and 'profile components' are rarely used, but a brief summary of the national curriculum in science is given in the appendix (p.173). We have, however, adopted the new nomenclature for the different age groups, running from Y1 for the 5–6 year olds to Y11 for 15–16 year olds for compulsory education and Y12 and Y13 for the years when students may stay on in schools in a voluntary capacity.

A useful source of advice for beginning teachers is of course the students in schools. They spend 5 hours a day, 39 weeks a year, for 11 years in school. They are remarkably perceptive about teachers and teaching and will provide any beginner teacher with a useful list of advice. They often try to analyse why they learn from some teachers and not from others. Conversations with them, as much as with beginning teachers, have convinced us of the value of finding a variety of ways of talking about teaching. Our hope is that this book makes some little contribution in the field, and will be useful to anyone reflecting on the art of teaching.

References

Black, P. (1987) 'Deciding to Teach' *STEAM* Issue No.8, ICI

Centre for Science Education, Sheffield City Polytechnic (1992) *Active Teaching and Learning Approaches in Science*, London: Collins Education

Driver, R. (1983) *The Pupil as Scientist*, Milton Keynes: Open University Press

Driver, R., Guesne, E., Tinberghien, A. (eds) (1985) *Children's Ideas in Science*, Milton Keynes: Open University Press

Gauld, C. 'A Study of Pupils' Responses to Empirical Evidence' Chapter 3 in R. Millar (ed.) (1989) *Doing Science: Images of Science in Science Education*, London: Falmer Press

Millar, R. and Driver, R. (1987) 'Beyond process' in *Studies in Science Education* 14, 33-62

Nuffield Foundation (1966) *Nuffield O Level Physics Teachers Guides 1–5*, London: Longmans

Nussbaum, G. (1985) 'The Earth as a Cosmic Body', Chapter 9 in Driver, Guesne, Tinberghien

Osborne, R. and Freyberg, P. (1985) *Learning in Science*, Auckland: Heinemann

Solomon, J. (1980) *Teaching Children in the Laboratory*, London: Croom Helm

Tobin, K., Butler Kahle, J., Fraser, B. J. (eds) (1990) *Windows into Science Classrooms*, Lewes: Falmer Press

Westaway, F. W. (1929) *Science Teaching*, London: Blackie

Woolnough, B. and Allsop, T. (1985) *Practical Work in Science*, Cambridge: Cambridge University Press

Wragg, E. C. (ed.) (1984) *Classroom Teaching Skills*, Croom Helm (reprinted 1986)

Further Reading

Bentley, D. and Watts, D. (1989) *Learning & Teaching in School Science: Practical Alternatives*, Milton Keynes: Open University Press

Brown, J., Cooper, A., Horton, T., Toates, F. and Zedlin, D. (1986) *Exploring the Curriculum: Science in Schools* , Milton Keynes: Open University Press

Fensham, P. (ed.) (1988) *Development and Dilemmas in Science Education*, London: Falmer Press.

Hull, R. (1993) *ASE Science Teachers Handbook, Secondary* Hemel Hempstead: Simon and Schuster

Ingle, R., Jennings, A. (1981) *Science in Schools, Which Way Now?*, University of London, Institute of Education

Levinson, R. (ed.) (1994) *Teaching Science* (Open University Reader), London,: Routledge

NCC (1993) *Teaching Science at Key Stages 3 and 4*, York: National Curriculum Council

Parkinson, J. (1994) *The Effective Teaching of Secondary Science*, London and New York: Longman

Rowland, S. (1984) *The Enquiring Classroom*, Lewes: Falmer Press

Woolnough, B. (1994) *Effective Science Teaching*, Buckingham: Open University Press

Notes

1. The use of the term 'beginning teacher' instead of 'student' to denote people in an initial professional course for teachers is now becoming fairly widespread.

2. The phrase 'teacher education' is more frequently used by those people who run courses because the word 'training' implies transfer of skills by straightforward instruction and demonstration, with practice exercises to follow. The process of learning to teach is far too complex for this type of training. The phrase 'teacher training' is however used more colloquially, for professional courses.

3. From September 1992 all courses of initial teacher education are to be planned and implemented through an equal partnership between schools and Institutions of Higher Education. While higher education will continue to carry the responsibility for quality assurance of the courses, teachers will play a larger part than hitherto in the 'delivery' (see Department for Education, Circular 9/92).

2
TEACHING SKILLS

Arthur Jennings

Making sense of science lessons

When taken on a tour of the school science laboratories during ordinary lesson time, a new parent or school governor with no particular knowledge of science education may emerge a little bewildered by the many different kinds of activities that are taking place. In some lessons not only are students seen to be working in small groups but the groups are engaged in different tasks. A short visit may reveal little of the overall purpose of a lesson and a sceptical person might ask whether all the activities are intentional and have doubts about what the children are learning. The situation is more complex because science lessons often occupy double or even treble timetable periods. Lessons of such extended duration require the teacher to know when an activity has run its useful course and to be adept at effecting a change of demand upon the students.

That school science laboratories are required to be very specialised, multi-media learning environments has been ruefully commented on by Stepan (1965) of the Architects and Building Branch, DES, who noted that students' practical work, teachers' demonstrations and direct lecturing may take place in the same teaching space rather than in neatly separated areas:

> From the designer's point of view this separation is just what he wants, or rather what he is trained to provide without much trouble. The brief is simple, the activities are well defined. Moreover, his mental pictures of a lecture room, a demonstration room and a laboratory are quite recent, clear and precise. There is something very satisfying about this order and harmony.
>
> Unfortunately very few teachers want such a separation of activities; they really want some sort of bedlam, in which anything may happen at any moment. Teachers claim that they may start with a straightforward lecture, suddenly decide to illustrate it with some slides or a demonstration and even break into a general chaos of a practical free-for-all. They claim that education at its best is a dynamic, creative process – a chain reaction; to force it into separate compartments (however neat and perfect) imposes considerable, if not intolerable, limitations on most fruitful teaching situations. (Stepan, 1965, pp.20–21)

Words such as 'creative' and 'dynamic' have an essentially educational ring, yet they may be construed as antithetical to 'organised' and 'planned'. Science teachers quickly learn that a disorganised laboratory class puts everyone at risk. Equally quickly beginning science teachers discover that dynamic and interesting learning activities, even in a subject as potentially exciting as science, require considerable imaginative and creative thought. Advance planning, careful organisation of materials and management of students can help to establish laboratory habits and practices which may pave the way for flexibility and response to students' ideas without ever transcending safety parameters. The apparent 'sort of bedlam' described by Stepan may, in fact, be an intended and skilfully controlled sequence of experiences and thought-provoking activities devised to stimulate and generate students' learning. The more professionally skilled teacher may be able to disguise the conscientious preparation and planning by the apparent easy informality and harmonious personal relationships in which the laboratory discourse proceeds.

Just as the architects need to identify the separate activities to be undertaken in the laboratory which they are to design, so science teachers need to think about component episodes of lessons. Each episode should make a particular contribution to students' learning and each will demand particular skills of the teacher. Successful synthesis of these episodes into a coherent set of learning experiences spanning the time of the lesson depends not only upon prior planning but upon skills of management and adaptability during the lesson. Stated in different terms, it is being suggested that the science teacher goes to the lesson with a clear set of learning goals for the students. During the lesson the teacher will be concerned with the achievement of these objectives. However, all the teacher's efforts should not simply be focused on driving the class along a predetermined route but, by monitoring students' responses and achievements, the teacher will need to moderate the planned programme to accommodate the situation as it develops. Discovering what learning outcomes are achieved and assessing these against intended outcomes will be further considered on pp.26 and 169–71.

Good science teaching involves more than being able to produce separate stimulating science lessons. For learning purposes the complex integrated world of science, with its matrix of great ideas, has to be broken down into discrete, manageable units. By themselves the objectives and learning outcomes of any one lesson may appear trivial, just as a single piece of a jigsaw puzzle appears insignificant. The teacher can help students to see relevance in the pieces by setting a lesson in a context which is meaningful to the learners. This only happens when the teacher has the necessary perspective including appreciation that there are significant gender differences as to meaningful contexts, is clear about the long-term goals of science education and understands how any one particular lesson contributes to the overall aims. New teachers often find it difficult to formulate clearly these long-term ends but they may be assisted by the advent of a national curriculum with prescribed levels of attainment and suggested programmes of study.

The *Report of the Science Working Group for the National Curriculum* (DES, 1988) set out a philosophy of science for all. Although National Curriculum Science has changed considerably since the Working Group's original proposals (DES, 1989, DES, 1991) the approach recommended in the original formative document remains valid. This approach needs to be embraced by science teachers who should each develop a personal sense of identity with, and ownership of, the science which is cryptically described in statutes. This scientific knowledge and orientation will have to be underpinned by teaching which recognises the way individuals learn. In practice this often means that a teacher may construct a lesson which has multiple objectives. Thus while students are studying the essential features of an electrical circuit they may also be practising investigation skills and, through exploratory talk, beginning to construct their own scientific models and thereby to gain a better understanding of the nature of science. There will be times in science lessons when the scientific matter that forms the focus of action is really no more than a vehicle for the development by the students of manipulative or thinking skills which are far more significant than the object of their practical activity. Thus students testing the strength and suitability for their purpose of different plastic bags may learn something about plastics and about design but more importantly may discover the value of accurate measurement, accurate recording, changing one variable at a time and the components of a fair test.

The casual visitor with whom we began this chapter will probably form opinions as to whether the teaching is good, bad or indifferent. Such judgements are likely to be superficial and ill-informed. Considerable educational experience and expertise is necessary in order to 'read' classroom interactions in depth. Teachers adopt different personal styles. While one teacher is constantly seen as the dynamic centre of attention whose personality commands the classroom, another is quiet and unobtrusive yet has the knack of always being on hand when help is needed. One teacher's voice is a constant part of the classroom scene but another is heard only intermittently. Such contrasting styles may be equally effective if these teachers with different personalities and gifts have a sufficient repertoire of skills.

In later chapters we shall explore in detail several contrasting teaching strategies and the essential skills for the adoption of each strategy. But first we shall take a brief look behind a few very common science lesson activities which our visitor will easily recognise. We shall scratch the surface of these episodes sufficient to show that the teacher is probably employing many skills which are not immediately obvious. As with many highly professional tasks, the better the teaching, the easier it appears.

Episodes in science lessons

We shall look into science lessons through a series of episodes. In each case we shall pose questions of the kind an interested visitor might ask and we shall briefly examine possibilities. We shall keep two perspectives in mind: first, what is the teacher's intention and how is the intended learning encouraged, and second, what demand is being made on the students and what learning is occurring. The episodes described are:

1. The teacher asks questions;
2. The teacher gives a demonstration;
3. The teacher gives an exposition;
4. Pupils watch a videotape;
5. Pupils report on their investigations;
6. The teacher marks students' work.

Episode 1   The teacher asks questions

The teacher in plate 2.1 is addressing questions to the whole class and students are signalling their readiness to respond. What kind of questions are being asked? Who answers? What purpose is served? What are students learning?

The teacher may simply be asking for recall of events of a previous lesson as a means of linking one lesson with the next, such as:

'What were the fuels you used during the energy circus last lesson?'
'What chemicals did we use to make carbon dioxide last week?'

Beginning with a few instances of factual recall the teacher's questions may move on to probe levels of understanding. In responding to students' answers the teacher may summarise key ideas on board or screen as well as asking supplementary questions to seek development of answers. The apparently simple device of asking questions to link lessons may in fact become a diagnostic tool to establish not just what has been remembered but what is understood. The base-line for the next learning sequence is being exposed.

Observation of question and answer sessions will reveal quite different purposes. Some questions seek recall of memorised material. When a teacher asks students for the common name for sodium chloride the question is a closed question in that there is only one correct answer. Closed questions are useful as a quick means of oral testing but what is to be done about those students who give answers which they thought were correct until told otherwise by the teacher? Is there time for remedial work to correct ideas or are these students left

Plate 2.1 The teacher asks questions

feeling puzzled or even rejected? If closed questions are a dominant feature of a teacher's questioning repertoire, this may convey a message that science deals primarily with topics which have 'right answers'.

Other questions present students with opportunities to offer explanations, project ideas and express their own opinions. These questions are open questions because the teacher is not expecting a single 'right' answer:

> 'How could we find out the best conditions to germinate parsley seeds?'
> 'How can we find out if our local river is affected by any kind of pollution?'

Open questions of this kind may be used to elicit students' explanations of scientific phenomena, may invite solutions to a problem, may lead to the formulation of a hypothesis or the design of an experimental procedure.

Open questions subtly change the status of teacher and learner. When closed questions are asked the teacher has a correct answer in mind and the students are interrogated. The teacher encourages those who respond correctly and with degrees of response ranging from gentleness through to exasperation indicates when misinformation is supplied. Answers to open questions merit more careful evaluation. A seemingly obtuse suggestion may prove to be fruitful for further investigation and a child's idea may be as good or better than a suggestion by the teacher.

While asking questions and responding to answers the teacher has opportunity to develop several further skills and insights. If questions are merely addressed to individuals who then speak to the teacher, the lesson fails to become a group activity but degenerates into a sequence of personal conversations. Good questioning involves the whole class and the teacher skilfully balances responses from girls and boys and students of different ability. The teacher will be mindful of the pace of progression so that interest is not lost but patient enough to allow time for the question to be decoded by the listener, for words to be formulated into an answer and sufficiently skilled at listening to hear the message even though the sequence of words uttered by the student may suggest something different. A teacher who knows the students well will know when to praise a response, when to press for more precision and when to plant a question on a particular student as a means of social control.

It is frequently asserted that science education promotes inquiring minds. The questions a teacher asks may serve this function but probably only if the teacher is a person whose sense of curiosity is still alive. The questions asked often give powerful clues to the teacher's view of science. Listening to the language used by teacher and by students will reveal whether genuine communication is occurring or whether there is a language discontinuity in which students struggle to mimic teachers' words but use them without understanding. Teaching science necessarily involves learning scientific terms but also involves learning to use everyday words with a scientific precision and a teacher engaged in a question and answer session will inevitably reveal their awareness of the level of language discourse. Further development of this language dimension is found in Chapter 8 on discussions.

Episode 2 The teacher gives a demonstration

Why has the teacher in plate 2.2 chosen to demonstrate? What makes for a good demonstration? What are students learning?

At the start of the lesson the teacher has carefully positioned the class so that every student has a clear view of the bench on which is a piece of apparatus unfamiliar to the boys (plate 2.3). Though the Van der Graaf generator is to be the focus of the demonstration the teacher assumes that the class has some familiarity with electrostatic phenomena encountered in everyday life. From time to time in school she has seen a student rub an inflated balloon on a woollen pullover and then suspend the balloon on a ceiling or vertical wall so she begins to draw on students' experience by a series of questions, such as: 'Has anyone got out of a car and suffered a slight electric shock when closing the door?'

Having anticipated the range of students' experiences she is able to elicit a wealth of background material about their knowledge and explanations of electrostatics. Then she explains the essentials of the generator and how it builds up charge. Thus the mystery of the machine is removed and she begins to explore the nature of the 'charge'. Class involvement is sustained by securing a volunteer, who, suitably assured that there is no mortal danger to life or limb, agrees to be 'charged up'. Pupils are instructed to watch carefully for any signs that anything is happening to the boy. The picture registers their involvement which is further heightened when the boy's hair begins to stand on end (plate 2.4).

By a series of separate demonstrations the generator is used to answer different questions. Pupils are involved in posing the questions, interpreting results and participating, in turn, in performing the investigations.

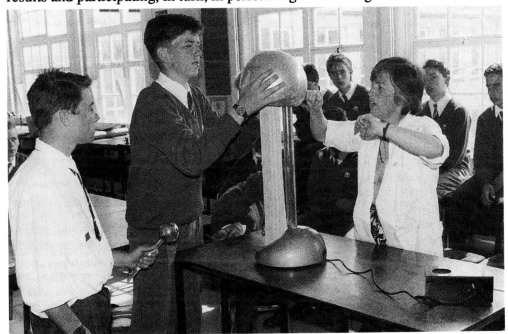

Plate 2.2 Demonstration of the Van der Graaf machine

Plate 2.3 Explaining that it is safe for a volunteer

Plate 2.4 A volunteer's hair begins to stand on end

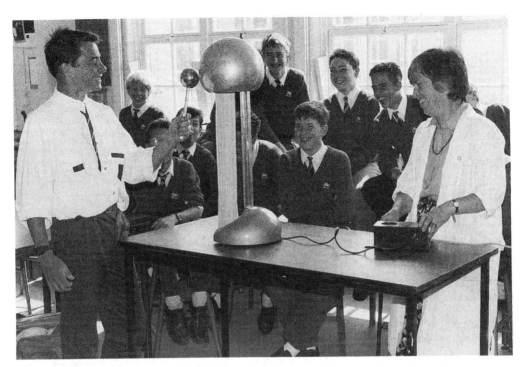

Plate 2.5 Charging via a sphere

Plate 2.6 Charge passing round the class

Can objects be charged? What kind of objects? Does the shape of the object matter? Can a 'charged up' student pass the charge on to another student? How many students can there be in the chain through which the charge will pass? (plates 2.5, 2.6)

Thus the demonstration lesson becomes an experiential learning occasion, an event not to be forgotten and a platform for further work and reflection.

Major demonstrations of the kind just described usually concentrate on a scientific reaction or a process to be investigated. The reason for a demonstration may be that the school has only one set of the necessary but expensive equipment or the work may involve use of reagents unsuitable for students to handle. For safety reasons it is sometimes necessary to perform the demonstration behind a screen or in a fume cupboard. Most teachers use such demonstrations infrequently and this allows the teacher to build up a sense of occasion, for a good demonstration becomes a piece of theatre. As with all demonstrations the teacher's practical skills are on view and students will inevitably form an opinion of the teacher as a practical scientist. Indeed, these skills need to be well practised because the demonstrator has to perform manipulative operations while maintaining a commentary but, here again, dull, flat statements will not engage attention or generate interest. A good demonstration will be supported by a narrative, a line of patter that focuses the attention of the observers on pertinent details and leads up to, but does not anticipate, the climax. In certain situations engagement of the audience may be intensified by inviting students to predict the outcome while on other occasions the element of surprise may help to ensure that the demonstration lives vividly in the memory. Because students watching a demonstration are freed from demands on their attention of manipulation of apparatus they can concentrate on theoretical scientific aspects. In this they can be helped by the teacher's discourse and questions and responsiveness to their contributions.

A good demonstration is enjoyable for students and satisfying for the teacher, but it is but one event in a learning sequence. The visual images, emotional engagement and intellectual stimulation need to be capitalised in the follow-up. So often students are merely told to move back to their regular places where they have to 'write up' what they have seen. The more expert the demonstration, the greater the let-down of such an unimaginative follow-up. There will be occasions when a written record of a demonstrated reaction or experiment will be essential but the form, timing and context of this record-making deserves as much attention as the demonstration itself.

There are other reasons why a teacher may elect to give a demonstration. From time to time students have to be shown how to perform a laboratory technique and a short demonstration is one way of helping students to learn a skill, as in plate 2.7 where the teacher is demonstrating the end point of a chemical reaction.

To watch a group of eleven-year-olds as they try for the first time to assemble a retort stand with boss and clamp is to appreciate that many manipulative tasks are not easy. Being shown how to do something safely and then having chance to practise is a necessary ingredient of science lessons. Time for student practice is vital and the teacher demonstration needs to be done expeditiously but clearly, and with accuracy. For these reasons it is essential to

Plate 2.7 Demonstrating the end point of a chemical reaction

have all the equipment ready to hand and to seat students so that they all have good sight of what is to be demonstrated. The teacher's knowledge of individual students will enable particular attention to be given to the position of any student with impaired sight. The task then needs to be performed meticulously with a commentary which focuses attention on every significant detail. Sometimes it will be desirable for the teacher to use a scaled-up model of the apparatus students will subsequently use so that everyone can see what has to be done. Thus, learning how to place a coverslip on a temporary slide preparation may first be demonstrated with two proportionately larger pieces of glass and then with the genuine articles. The teacher should always stress any safety considerations but without overstatement so that more cautious students do not become fearful of undertaking the task.

After seeing a task performed, even well performed, students often find it difficult to replicate the steps. Teachers quickly learn the points at which children are likely to go wrong and it is sometimes helpful at the end of a teacher demonstration to invite one student to perform the task while other students watch. When a teacher demonstrates how to inoculate an agar plate it all seems simple; the lid of the petri dish is to be lifted a little, the spreader sterilised, dipped into the inoculum and then moved over the surface of the agar without ploughing deep furrows before the lid is placed back in position. The beginner soon discovers that three hands seem to be necessary to prevent dropping the lid or the agar plate becoming chopped by the impact of the spreader. Therefore, before students leave their demonstration positions it is advisable to ensure that there is a written summary on board, screen or worksheet about key practical points.

When students begin their practical work the teacher becomes an observer and an assistant to those having difficulty. During a demonstration by the teacher students are engaged in making a visual recording of what the teacher does but their practical work involves a translation of this 'knowledge' into a routine of manipulative movements which are perhaps being performed for the first time. This kind of activity presents the student with a mental demand as well as a physical demand. Concentration on doing the task may deflect the student from considering the reason for performing the task in the first place. Increasingly teachers are coming to appreciate that to expect students to perform a practical activity as a means to elucidate theoretical principles, while simultaneously acquiring new manipulative skills as an accidental spin-off, is to set unrealistic goals (Woolnough and Allsop, 1985).

Episode 3   The teacher gives an exposition

When is exposition appropriate? How does the teacher hold students' attention? What kind of follow-up? What are students learning?

The teacher stands before the class, addressing the students. On this occasion the subject is the pumping action of a mammalian heart. Similar to a demonstration but lacking the apparatus and practical dimension, the teacher holds attention by skilled delivery and adept use of model and chart.

Listening in to the exposition we shall hear the teacher giving information which is detailed, orderly and systematic. Movements of the chambers on the right side of the heart are described and then the left side both illustrated by hand movements and simulated sounds of heart valves. Throughout, the teacher communicates not just by word of mouth, but by eye contact and facial expression.

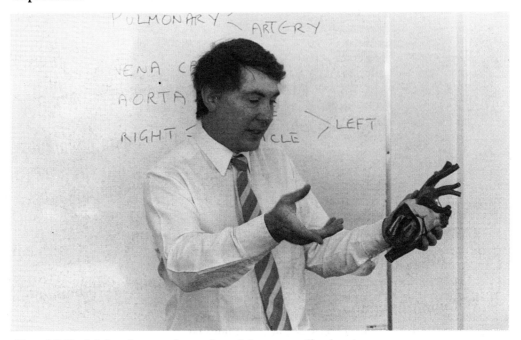

Plate 2.8 Explaining the pumping action of the mammalian heart

This looks and sounds like teaching everyone has experienced. Is not this kind of formal, didactic presentation old-fashioned and discredited as mere transmission? Experienced teachers know that there are topics, often of a detailed and theoretical nature, when student discovery approaches are inappropriate. On occasions historical anecdote or biographical detail provide the vital context which shows science to be a creative activity in which progress has been erratic or intermittent. Human beings enjoy a story. A teacher with a well-prepared, interestingly told explanatory discourse can hold the attention of students with a minimum of visual aids for several minutes. Notice in the picture that a word summary is being built up as the sequence unfolds. Pupils are required to give the whole of their attention to the narrative so must be seated near to the teacher so that there is a closeness of contact; in this arena teaching aids are clearly visible and a nod or a frown may effectively signal to individuals whose attention has begun to wander. Meanwhile, note-books have to be well out of reach so that no student is tempted to pay more attention to writing than listening. Follow-up will involve hearing heart valves in action, watching animated film to show heart movements and note-making.

The teacher is endeavouring to enable students to understand heart action. The details are complex involving muscle contraction and relaxation, heart chambers filling and emptying, valves to ensure one way flow of blood and synchronised action of right and left sides. Few students will gain a secure

Plate 2.9 Indicating the valves and explaining their function

knowledge from the teacher's exposition alone and there will need to be a programme of further activities to follow up the exposition. Indeed, the teacher may choose to present a simplified story in the exposition, deliberately making it an introduction as a platform for work by the students who will begin to build their own notes as a result of practical work, reading and response to specific written questions in a study guide.

Especially at Y12 and 13 level there is often considerable expository teaching. While it is reasonable to prepare these older students for university lectures, the attempt by students to write down a rather full précis of what the teacher is saying may not be the best way to encourage learning. Nevertheless, at all levels, teachers should not feel guilty about giving an exposition. Good presentation by a teacher can generate interest, anticipate points of conceptual difficulty, direct listeners to good sources of information or articulate areas of controversy. Badly used expository teaching can narrow students' horizons by giving the impression that the teacher knows all the answers and thereby suggesting that success in science equates with learning these right answers.

Episode 4   Pupils watch a videotape

Why has this medium been chosen? Is this passive watching or active learning? What kind of follow-up is required?

Many science teachers use videotape as a valuable teaching resource. These Y11 students are watching a programme which relates Newton's understanding of forces to the flight and manœuvring of the space shuttle. Although the programme sequence lasts twenty minutes the teacher has decided to show the

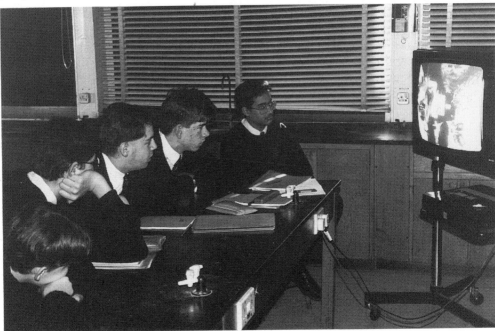

Plate 2.10 Group watching a videotape 'Newton and the space shuttle'

whole programme. The students have already encountered the essential background theory and with few preliminaries the class watch the programme.

When the programme ends the teacher asks questions to elicit from students those aspects of the film that have made a strong impression. Human factors about safety, weightlessness, including problems of feeding and movement, feature prominently in students' minds but the teacher's primary purpose concerns forces and so there begins a process of redirection as the teacher compiles a set of questions. Some students suggest answers based on their memory of the programme but others volunteer ideas which are contradictory. These differences of opinion help to create a readiness for a second viewing but this time students are armed with questions which focus their attention. From time to time during the second viewing the programme is stopped for the teacher to elaborate a point and to allow students to write their own notes. In practice the teacher is carrying out a modified DARTS (Directed Activities Related to Text) procedure, except that in this situation students are interrogating a television 'text' (Bulman, 1985; Davies and Greene, 1984).

Television is a powerful medium. Experts from many scientific fields can be brought into the classroom and, conversely, students can be transported through visual and aural experiences to situations and events in many different parts of the world. Quality of picture and speech is usually excellent because a skilled production team has carefully selected from a mass of material to compile a concentrated piece of informative viewing. By comparison the science teacher's unscripted lesson sequences may seem pedestrian but for learning purposes much videotape contains an acute information overload. The teacher needs to select appropriate passages and to decide when to turn down the sound and give a live commentary more suited to the class.

Appearance on video of scientists speaking about their personal research can help students to understand science as a human activity. Occasionally different researchers may be shown giving different interpretations of the same event or phenomenon and this is a useful way to expose students to the way scientists engage in debate and search for truth. However, it is more common to find film in which scientists speak confidently about their work and the message comes across as one of authority and authenticity. All too often this real science appears irrefutable and devoid of any controversial element. To counter this impression the teacher may choose, from time to time, to juxtapose a video sequence with evidence presented in a different form. An example of this strategy was used when some Y13 students watched a video sequence from a schools television series on evolution. A researcher was seen trapping long-tailed field mice on remote Scottish Islands and proceeded to demonstrate differences between races of the same species. These differences, it was argued, illustrate stages towards evolution of separate species due to selection acting in isolated communities. The Y13 students were also supplied with a paper from a scientific journal in which the author presented the case for a theory of spontaneous eruption to explain island populations of similar species. The students were required to evaluate the evidence of both presentations and to seek other sources of information before drawing their own conclusions.

Television is associated in students' minds with entertainment. Good educational programmes should also be enjoyable and much informal learning will occur when students give their attention to viewing. Nevertheless, the teacher will have a very specific reason for selecting the tape. A film may be chosen to introduce a topic or alternatively used for consolidation or revision. There are also parts of the science curriculum which can only be dealt with by second-hand experience, and then a videotape may provide the best substitute for the real thing. As we have already seen with respect to teacher demonstrations, follow-up to an entertaining activity has to be planned carefully, otherwise students may over-react because what is perceived as a 'work' activity follows a 'leisure' activity.

Episode 5   Students report on their investigations

Why are the students addressing the class in plate 2.11? What are students learning? What is the teacher doing? Does this require skill on the part of the teacher? Three Y10 students are reporting on their investigation. One tells how, over the past few lessons, they have made a chemical clock to measure as accurately as they can a time delay of one minute. The process involved mixing sodium thiosulphate solution and dilute hydrochloric acid in a flask to form an opaque solution so that a cross marked on paper underneath the flask became invisible when viewed through the mixture. A second student takes up the story and explains how they changed the amounts of acid and tried to make adjustments to the reaction time by diluting the concentration of the acid. They

Plate 2.11 Students reporting on an investigation

also showed, by using a large graph prepared for the class to see, the effect of changing the temperature on the rate of the reaction.

In telling their story the students reveal that they began their investigation with a trial and error approach. They were eager to find out what happened when the two reagents were mixed. They discovered that they could produce a very quick reaction but in their enthusiasm they changed the amounts of both reagents in successive reactions. This, they said, had wasted their time and so they decided to work systematically. They then kept the volume of thiosulphate solution constant and varied the amount of acid. With a little help from the teacher they saw how they could translate their data on the amount of acid and reaction time into a graph from which it was possible to predict the quantity of acid to produce a one-minute reaction.

Students who listened to this account asked questions and some explained how their investigations, although on different topics, had shown a similar need to change one variable at a time. Other contributions began to explore further avenues of investigation and applications of the principles of reaction time that had been discovered.

Why had the teacher chosen to invite students to report to the class? Were the students asked to write an account of their investigation? Is the teacher employing a teaching skill at all or taking an easy option? In practice the teacher was using several subtle devices to develop the students' scientific skills and learning. The young reporters had written a report, but the requirement to give an oral account to their contemporaries sharpened their focus. They were alive to the need to be accurate in describing what they had done, to state what kind of results had been recorded and to ensure that their conclusion was reliable. Indeed, they decided that they had sufficient confidence in their work to demonstrate their one-minute chemical timer. Therefore by the device of class reporting the teacher has enriched the learning potential of carrying out an investigation. Accountability to their peers intensified attention to accuracy and the need for replication to ensure reliability. Thought about presentation paved the way for confidence when engaged in reporting to the class and while some of the presentation was scripted, response to questions was spontaneous. Interaction of the three presenters was mutually supportive.

A very significant skill on the part of the teacher lies behind the success of this style of class work. Over a lengthy period of time this teacher had encouraged students to listen to each other and from cautious beginnings had developed a climate for collaborative learning. Short discussions generated by students' investigation reports began to lead to explicit articulation of some of the higher level investigation skills set out in Attainment Target 1 of the National Curriculum Science and other parts of the discussion elucidated aspects of the nature of science.

The teacher was also listening carefully as students reported and engaged in discussion, so detecting clues about the depth, breadth and limits of students' understanding. Evidence of students' frameworks was noted and indications of unresolved problems about performing investigations were recorded for later attention. Thus the teacher gained evaluative information about students' levels of attainment in process skills, cognitive attainment and also about the more elusive, affective dimension of social skills. In these circumstances the teacher is entitled to believe that the extra time given to occasional use of this form of class activity is time well spent.

Episode 6   The teacher marks students' work

What skills are involved? What do the students learn from the teacher's comments?

As students perform their practical work and write an account of their activities, the teacher moves around the laboratory both assisting with the practical and looking at students' written work. This teacher expects students to write their definitive account immediately rather than to make rough jottings ready for a more orderly account to be written later. The teacher's inspection of what is being written is not to award a mark or grade but to offer oral or written comment. The teacher ensures that scientific terms are correctly spelt, points out if the sequential order of the account is misleading, makes constructive suggestions about ways to proceed and gives encouragement when work is shaping up well or causing frustration. Most important is that the teacher is showing an interest in what each student is doing and by involvement in each students' personal account, maintains a concern for accuracy which characterises reporting in science. These exchanges between student and teacher, focused on the practical and recording, allow the teacher to share as a participant in the work while at the same time indicating acceptable standards and encouraging students towards realistic expectations for their own attainments.

Plate 2.12 Marking a student's work

The teacher is conscious that this kind of attention to individual and group work and their written records fashions the work climate of the class in the laboratory. Stated in other terms, 'marking' students' classwork as it is being done is an element of good management. Laboratory discipline is achieved and reinforced not by coercion but by engagement with students in their action, thinking and recording.

Much marking of students' work has to be done outside lesson time but, with prior thought, marking can involve the teacher in a variety of different activities. We have already noted how important it is at the lesson planning stage for the teacher to give thought to the intended learning. Often the learning process will involve a written element, but it is essential for the teacher to be clear about the purpose of this writing. Is the writing an opportunity to clarify ideas or to deploy an argument or to compile a list? Students need to undertake tasks which develop different skills and which give opportunity for individuals to show flair and initiative. Some students respond best to a highly structured format while others enjoy a greater degree of freedom. From time to time students may be given a week or two in which to compile a substantial piece of work but the teacher has to be mindful of the volume of marking being generated by different classes so that several classes do not simultaneously submit lengthy pieces.

Marking has traditionally involved the teacher operating as an assessor, resulting in the award of a mark or grade to each piece of work. This is now seen as but one approach to marking though the teacher will always be concerned about learning outcomes. Students like to feel that their work is valued and taken seriously, but many discover a new freedom when given opportunity to write for an audience other than the teacher as assessor. Writing a scientific piece for the school magazine, a letter to a newspaper or a proposal for the design of a new product to a manufacturer may enable students to set their scientific understanding in a real-life context. It also allows the teacher to 'mark' by responding from the standpoint of the recipient. Some students show an imagination which surprises their teachers when invited to do a piece of creative writing. One fourteen-year-old girl, when asked to give an account of the carbon cycle written as though she was a carbon atom, handed in a piece entitled 'My Life Story' by Carbon Atom, which amazed her teacher by the completeness of the scientific story and insights which had never before been revealed in her attempts at formal scientific writing.

Given that the teacher sets students work which involves practice of different skills, 'marking' may involve the teacher in:

- checking lists and work completion exercises
- appraising diagrams and drawing skills
- recording students' alternative frameworks
- monitoring students' language registers
- editing students' articles and responding briefly to letters
- assessing students' attempts at analysis or synthesis
- diagnosing misconceptions that indicate the need for further teaching
- recognising students' achievements when measured against attainment targets.

More important than grading in all these appraisals is the relation between the teacher and the student. Each mark or teacher's comment may encourage and motivate or diminish and discourage the student. Sometimes the teacher will have set differentiated tasks to students of different ability and marking skills often involve a form of 'matching' skill in which the teacher, informed about students' age, ability and past achievements, seeks to respond appropriately to both the effort the learner has put into the work as well as to the scientific attainment which it reveals.

Summary

During the hour or thereabouts of a science lesson, students may be engaged in several distinct kinds of activity. Good science teaching requires the teacher to have a repertoire of skills from which to select in order to initiate and manage these different activities. Additionally the teacher needs to be able to co-ordinate these component episodes or parts of a lesson into a cumulative, rich learning experience for students.

References

Bulman, L. (1985) *Teaching Language and Study Skills in Secondary Science*, London: Heinemann Educational

Davies, F. and Greene, T. (1984) *Reading for Learning in the Sciences*, Edinburgh: Oliver and Boyd for the Schools Council

DES (1988) *Science for Ages 5–16 Proposals for the Secretary of State for Education and Science and the Secretary of State for Wales*, London: HMSO

DES (1989) *Science in the National Curriculum*, London: HMSO

DES (1991) *Science in the National Curriculum*, London: HMSO

Stepan, O. (1965) 'The design of biological laboratories for secondary schools' in Wyatt, H.V. (ed.) *The Design of Biological Laboratories*, London: Institute of Biology

Woolnough, B. and Allsop, T. (1985) *Practical Work in Science*, Cambridge: Cambridge Educational

3
PRACTICAL WORK
Jenny Frost

School laboratories and their messages

School science rooms and their apparatus, especially in the UK, reveal a long-held belief in the value of practical work in learning science. The rooms, to some extent, resemble science laboratories in industry. There is water for making up solutions, mains electricity for operating a range of equipment, and gas for heating substances. Workbenches imply messy experimentation; they are of a height suitable for standing and working, with stools to allow sitting, when appropriate. Some variations on this description do occur (lower level for benches; flexible arrangement of furniture as an alternative to the serried ranks of benches), but the essential features remain in most schools.

Uniformity and simplicity are built into the apparatus. Test tubes, flasks and beakers are mass-produced; they are made out of Pyrex which does not melt, does not react with chemicals or absorb solutions. In other words, variables, which might distort the results of an experiment, are already controlled at the manufacturing stage, and the need for this is taken for granted.

There are measuring instruments for weight, mass, length, volume, voltage, current, temperature, pressure, time; there are scales, dials and digital displays to be read. Increasingly electronic measuring equipment can be found, as well as electronic data-logging devices. There may well be facilities for connecting equipment to a computer so that readings can be taken and plotted automatically. There are cutting tools; tools for transferring liquids and solids from one container to another; retort stands for holding elaborate assemblages of apparatus; electrical water baths and incubators for maintaining cultures at given temperatures; aids to visual observation such as hand lenses and microscopes; power packs to give a range of voltages.

Unlike industrial laboratories there are of course class sets of apparatus to initiate everyone at the same time into the same experimental procedure. There is also the equipment designed specifically to explain or demonstrate a particular feature or phenomenon: evacuated tubes to demonstrate the rectilinear propagation of electrons; ripple tanks to demonstrate properties of waves; apparatus for safely showing the diffusion of bromine. Added to the apparatus and equipment are the models 'explaining' our knowledge of different aspects of the natural world: models of atoms and molecules to show structure and chemical composition; models of the solar system; models of ears, eyes and skeletons.

All this automatically conveys a message about what constitutes science; it is a silent message which is taken for granted and is transmitted without teaching. I would not argue that this should not happen nor that practical work should not play a part in learning science; it does for instance plant the message that the prime court of appeal in science is observation, but it must be recognised that not all countries devote as much time and resources to practical science as the UK. The readings at the end of the chapter provide considerable coverage of debates on the contribution of practical work to learning in science, but some analysis of its role is essential here in order to understand the demands that practical work makes on both students and teachers.

Types of practical work

It is possible to label all activities in a science lesson involving equipment, tools and measuring instruments as 'practical' but this masks the different purposes that such activities serve, so some categorisation is helpful. Allsop and Woolnough (1985) distinguished three types of practical work which, they believe, can be justified in school science, namely:

a) exercises to develop practical skills and techniques;
b) problems and investigations to develop problem solving and investigative skills; and
c) experiences designed to 'get a feel for phenomena'.

Allsop and Woolnough explicitly excluded the use of practical work as a *key* instrument for the development of understanding of scientific theory. Their reasons are cogently argued in Chapter 3 of their book, but a summary is given here in the section, entitled 'The link between practical work and learning scientific theory' (p.54).

Gott and Foulds (1989) in their book on assessment of practical science, divided practical work into four broad types ('basic skills', 'observations', 'illustrations','investigations'), which are similar to the three above, except that Woolnough's and Allsop's 'experiences designed to get a feel for phenomena' are essentially divided into 'observation' and 'illustrative' practical work.

Gott and Foulds were part of the team of researchers, based at the University of Durham, who reported to the National Curriculum Council (NCC) on Investigative Work in Science (Foulds, Gott, and Feasey, 1991) and consequently their classification has been built into recent NCC documents, for instance, *Teaching Science at Key Stages 3 and 4* (NCC, 1993). This describes observation practical work as involving observation of an event or object (observation of cells; observation of rocks) either using the senses or senses augmented by tools such as hand lenses and microscopes. Activities such as classifying and comparing observations (comparing one rock with another, one type of cell with another) are regarded as an intrinsic part of such practical work. On the other hand, illustrative practical work involves illustrating a particular phenomenon, such as: setting up a stream bed to show that large stones are deposited by a stream sooner than small stones; and studying the effect of light levels on photosynthesis.

Basic skills and illustrative, practical work are characterised by having fairly tight constraints over what apparatus is to be used, how it is to be used, what is to be observed and what is to be recorded. They are often accompanied by step-by-step instructions. Observation activities can be a little more open-ended and exploratory, being used often to generate questions about the phenomenon or object under observation. Investigations, on the other hand, start with a fairly well defined question to investigate (sometimes set by the teacher, sometimes by the student), and require students to decide how they will proceed, what apparatus they will use, what they will measure, what and how they will record, how they will interpret the results and how they will evaluate the experiment.

To illustrate the types of practical work and describe the role of the teacher in each one, we followed several lessons, capturing what we could with photographs. Included in this chapter are one lesson which could be classified mainly as an 'exercise to develop basic practical skills' (a Y7 lesson on temperature change), one lesson which provided experiences to 'illustrate a phenomenon' (a Y9 lesson on fire-fighting) and one which was based on observation (a Y12 lesson on crayfish). We have also included photographs of a lesson which developed understanding of scientific theory to show the marked contrast with practical work (Y13 lesson on the wave theory of light), even though one or two practical experiences occurred in the lesson.

Lessons involving the fourth type of practical work, problems and investigations, are incorporated in Chapter 4 of this book which deals exclusively with this category. Interest in the use of this last category rose considerably in the 1980s with an increased focus in science education on the processes as well as the products of science and has become much more widespread in the last few years with the inclusion in the *National Curriculum in Science* (1991) of the use of whole investigations in science teaching and the use of technological tasks as part of the *National Curriculum in Technology* (1991).

Exercises to develop practical skills

Lesson 1: Temperature changes

Plates 3.1–3.15 were taken during a 50-minute lesson which was designed primarily to give students an opportunity to practise skills which they had learnt previously, namely: the ability to measure volume, temperature and time; to work collaboratively; to take care of equipment; to record results accurately and transfer these to a graph.

The photographs of the apparatus and blackboard set out before the lesson gave clues to the preparation necessary (plates 3.1, 3.3). A comparatively simple task had been selected that was within the conceptual understanding of the class and yet was not too trivial. The topic was 'change of state' and the particular lesson involved an exercise to monitor changes in water temperature after the addition of a piece of ice. With good organisation the exercise could be fitted into the limited time slot of 50 minutes. Sufficient apparatus had been ordered for the students to work in twos or threes and had been put in sensible places for collection (plate 3.3). The chart that was needed was on the blackboard. Registering students and returning books was done as quickly as possible so that the science could start (plates 3.2, 3.4). In the introduction to the lesson the teacher explained that he was providing an opportunity to practise skills and that he would be looking particularly for careful and proper use of the equipment and accurate measurement (plate 3.5).

Lesson 1   Temperature changes: a practical skills exercise

Plate 3.1 Class arriving; ice for experiment on the front bench

Plate 3.2 Class registration

Lesson 1   Temperature changes: a practical skills exercise (cont.)

Plate 3.3 Apparatus in sensible places for collection

Plate 3.4 Distributing marked books

He also talked about the phenomenon itself and asked the class to predict what was likely to happen to the temperature. Predicting served several functions. First, it tuned in the class to thinking about the phenomenon. Second, it helped the teacher to probe understanding. Third, it made explicit the sort of readings to expect and helped students identify sooner rather than later if they were getting quite spurious readings. It is important to remember that students, as novice experimenters, cannot easily distinguish between strange results from faulty apparatus or poor technique and genuine results.

The introduction also involved management: putting students into groups, organising for half the class to include a variation on the exercise, where they added a second piece of ice after five minutes; explaining what equipment was available and organising collection so that everyone did not crowd the same place at the same time. Plate 3.7 shows the precaution that the teacher took to distribute the more vulnerable glass thermometers himself once the students were settled.

Once this had been done the lesson moved to the next phase when students were undertaking measurements. The teacher went first to groups who might have difficulties and helped where necessary, but eventually visited all pairs (plates 3.8–3.9). Several groups stopped the clock after each minute while they took the temperature and this had to be corrected early on; many of the students did in fact realise for themselves that this was inappropriate to the task, but it illustrates that even a comparatively simple task requires careful planning and good co-operation between partners. The teacher reminded students of measuring techniques, for instance moving so that their eye was on a horizontal level with the appropriate points on the thermometer or measuring cylinder, and of the need to read the bottom of the meniscus, to be ready to record just as the clock reached the next minute, to record the results in the chart. Plates 3.10 and 3.11 show the concentration and the willingness of the students to work as accurately as possible. Throughout the activity the teacher kept an eye on the time and gave a time warning to the class to complete within the next five minutes (plate 3.12). Finally he organised clearing up, so that equipment was already stacked ready to be taken away quickly at the end of the lesson.

The final part of the lesson, was spent in discussing the sort of results obtained, looking at the range of temperatures from one or two groups (plate 3.13). The homework set was the task of transferring the results onto a graph and at the end of the lesson the teacher distributed the graph paper.

We did not photograph the next lesson but there are a range of possible directions it could have taken. Had marking the homework revealed difficulty in transferring data from table to graph, then practice in this skill might well have been the next step. If there had been no such difficulty then a fuller discussion of results could have ensued. The attention that had been paid to collecting results meant that there was something worth discussing. Were the graphs within each half of the class more or less the same? The answer would be yes, and this is a point which needs registering; it would indicate they had used the equipment correctly and made reasonable recordings. Were they identical? The answer would be no. Again it is worth discussing the possible reasons, which focus on the difficulty of everyone doing exactly the same or of having identical

Lesson 1 Temperature changes: a practical skills exercise (cont.)

Plate 3.5 Introduction; explanation of task; asking questions

Plate 3.6 Collection of apparatus and the required volume of water

Lesson 1   Temperature changes: a practical skills exercise (cont.)

Plate 3.7 Distributing the more vulnerable equipment

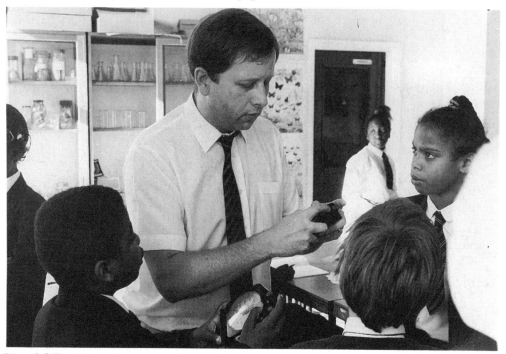

Plate 3.8 Explaining how to use the stopclock

Lesson 1 Temperature changes: a practical skills exercise (cont.)

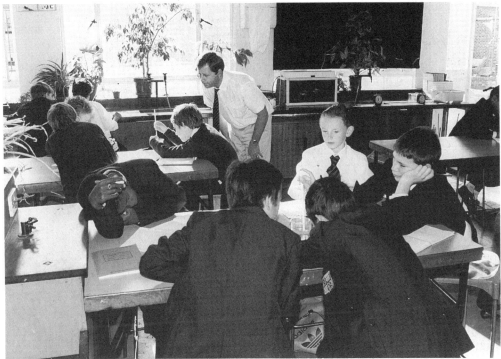

Plate 3.9 Checking procedures and readings

Plate 3.10 Concentration necessary for accuracy

Lesson 1   Temperature changes: a practical skills exercise (cont.)

Plate 3.11 Co-ordinating reading of thermometer and watch

Plate 3.12 Giving a time reminder

Lesson 1   Temperature changes: a practical skills exercise (cont.)

Plate 3.13 Collecting results from the two halves of the class

Plate 3.14 Listening to the summary

Plate 3.15 Exposition as part of the summary

conditions in one part of the room as another (some experiments were in bright sunshine, others in shade). What were the major differences between the groups that had added the second piece of ice later and the others? Could they explain the difference?

There is also the possibility of probing understanding a little further. Had the water cooled as much as they had expected? How does the water heat up once it has gone cold from the ice? How long does it take to heat up? Where does the heat come from? What would the final temperature be if it were left for a long time? These questions require speculation as well as straightforward interpretation of the results and require a different mode of teaching.

Are these exercises necessary? We believe they are. Most teachers recognise that into the simplified 'controlled' environment of a school laboratory we introduce the biggest variable of all, the students. They are not skilled in the craft knowledge of science nor in the practical skills of experimental scientists. It is all too easy to discover in a school laboratory that everyone, apparently doing the same thing, produces different results. Yet one of the tenets on which science is based is that experiments are repeatable and that the natural world is not capricious, behaving in one way today and another tomorrow. In fact the stability of the natural world is one of its attractions and one of the features which draws people to the study of science.

Unless students can become careful and skilled in the way they work, measure and record, they will lose sight of this stability. Ineptness will mask the phenomenon being studied. Training in practical skills can therefore be seen as a means of learning to 'capture' quietly and systematically information about the natural world. It would also replace the self-deprecating comments, such as 'It never works for me, so I write down what the teacher tells me is supposed to happen', by a personal confidence in their own skills and a pleasure in success.

If we are to encourage students to value their experimental data we need at least to minimise the variability brought into the lab by their own inexperience. The 'controlled' environment of the lab can be an expensive and irrelevant feature if some attention is not paid to training in practical skills. But above all, if students leave the lessons convinced of their own ability and aware of their developing skills then this is worthwhile. It reduces the chance of their seeing no point in doing practical of any sort because 'now it does work for them'.

Extending experience; illustrative practical work

In illustrative practical work teachers contrive to create practical experiences which show as clearly as possible particular phenomena. They will want the students to have first-hand experience of a phenomenon so that they can engage in discussion of both what is happening and the principles behind it.

First hand experience helps to build up what is often referred to as 'tacit knowledge'. It is the sort of knowledge that can be gained through practical hobbies such as gardening, sports, model-making, fishing, cooking, photography, carpentry, looking after pets or mending gadgets. But unless this knowledge is articulated it will remain at the tacit level, preventing the owner from extending his/her thinking to the principles involved. In providing for this

Lesson 2   Fire-fighting: illustrative practical work

Plate 3.16 Questioning as part of the introduction

Plate 3.17 Explaining practical and written tasks

type of learning therefore science teachers not only have to provide interesting ways for students to interact with phenomena they also have to create the conditions where ideas can be articulated and extended.

Lesson 2   Fire-fighting: illustrative practical work

We photographed a Y9 lesson on fire-fighting as an example of a lesson which could be classified as a practical lesson where teachers were extending students' experience, providing conditions in which the experience could be discussed, and hence creating opportunities to extend understanding.

Plates 3.16–3.32 show the lesson on fire extinguishers; the lesson started with a discussion of the fire triangle, summarising that a fire burns only if fuel, heat and oxygen are present and that exclusion of any one of these would stop the fire. The practical involved the use of two different sorts of fire extinguishers (water to reduce heat, and sand to isolate the fuel from the oxygen in the air) with the purpose of using the experience to consider the most suitable techniques for tackling a range of large fires including forest fires. A third type, a foam extinguisher, was demonstrated by the teacher; and students were to try this out for themselves in the next lesson.

The laboratory was relatively small and conditions were cramped, so good organisation and discipline were essential. Such conditions, coupled with the safety at work legislation, might persuade a teacher to use a demonstration but then students would lose the experience of handling fire safely. In making decisions like this a teacher has to bear in mind that the safest people are, on the whole, those who have been taught how to handle potentially dangerous situations properly rather than those who have never been exposed to them.

The preparation required ordering appropriate sets of apparatus which were placed at sensible places round the laboratory; a diagram was ready on the blackboard and the questions that the class had to address at the end were ready on an overhead projector transparency, as well as on printed sheets. When the students arrived they sat at their tables while the register was taken, after which they were brought round the front bench.

The teacher started by questioning the class about the significance of the fire triangle (plate 3.16). After discussing the fire triangle she explained that during the practical activities the students had to consider the effectiveness and practicality of two different methods of extinguishing fires (sand and water), and to use their ideas to answer questions about fire-fighting techniques. She inevitably gave safety warnings about behaviour necessary to ensure there were no accidents during the lesson, reminding the class of the need to tie back long hair and wear goggles. She then asked the students to go back to their places to copy drawings of the apparatus, leaving space for recording what happened. They also wrote the questions they would be trying to answer at the end. This was done partly to allow the teacher time to give out equipment and sort out individual problems (plates 3.18–3.20). This illustrates well the importance of planning the management of movement of students between different types of activities with considerable precision.

Lesson 2 Fire-fighting: illustrative practical work (cont.)

Plate 3.18 Distributing apparatus

Plate 3.19 Distributing apparatus provides an opportunity to check the start of written work

Lesson 2   Fire-fighting: illustrative practical work (cont.)

Plate 3.20 Responding to individual questions

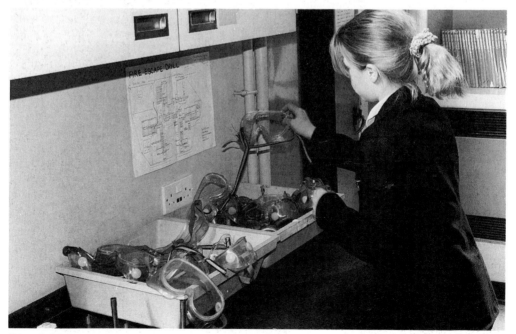

Plate 3.21 Student collecting safety goggles

Lesson 2   Fire-fighting: illustrative practical work (cont.)

Plate 3.22 Trying out the sand extinguisher

Plate 3.23 Keeping a watchful eye on fires

Lesson 2   Fire-fighting: illustrative practical work (cont.)

Plate 3.24 Responding to questions about fire fighting from aeroplanes

Plate 3.25 Students recording results and writing answers to questions

Lesson 2   Fire-fighting: illustrative practical work (cont.)

Plate 3.26 Sharing answers

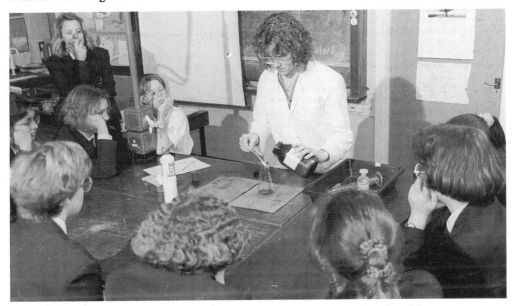

Plate 3.27 Demonstrating and explaining the construction of a foam extinguisher

Once students were trying out their fire extinguishers her role became mainly one of keeping an eye on the general organisation and safety, checking students had goggles, clarifying points on instructions, but also one of discussing with pairs what they observed, and how effective they thought the methods were (plates 3.22–3.24). As groups finished they cleared their benches and began considering answers to the questions (plate 3.25).

When everyone had had time to consider the questions, she brought the whole class together to listen to different pairs' thoughts about the effectiveness of various fire-fighting methods such as fire prevention corridors in forests, the use of aeroplanes spraying water or sand on forest fires (plate 3.29). In the final part of the lesson she demonstrated how to set up a model foam extinguisher (plates 3.27–3.30), using the opportunity to remind students of practical skills – hence plate 3.28 in which she reminds students to measure the bottom of the meniscus when measuring liquid in a measuring cylinder. This was to be repeated by the class at the start of the next lesson. Finally the class moved back to their seats and packed ready to leave the science laboratories (plates 3.31, 3.32).

This lesson illustrates well the point made by Stepan (see p.10) about the many purposes to which a laboratory is put; this laboratory was a place for questioning, whole class discussion, practical work done in pairs, individual writing and teacher demonstration. Consideration must be given at the planning stage to ways of minimising the time taken to change from one type of activity to another.

Lesson 2   Fire fighting: illustrative practical work (cont.)

Plate 3.28 Reminding the class of techniques while measuring out the required volume of water

Lesson 2 Fire fighting: illustrative practical work (cont.)

Plate 3.29 Explaining technique for transferring acid

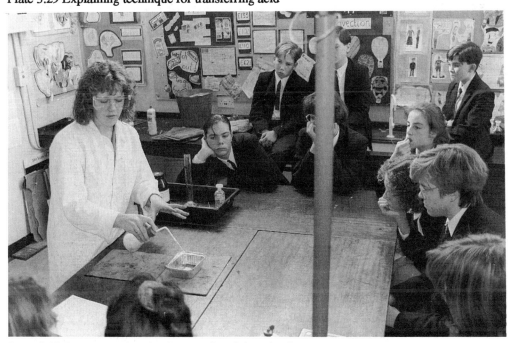

Plate 3.30 Demonstrating the foam extinguisher ejecting water

Lesson 2   Fire fighting: illustrative practical work (cont.)

Plate 3.31 Class returning to their seats

Plate 3.32 Ready to leave for the next lesson

Practical work based on observation

Lesson 3 A-level biology lesson: study of crayfish: observation practical work

In this example of an observation practical activity students at a tertiary college were asked to draw a picture of a crayfish from a preserved specimen (plates 3.33–3.37). The purpose of the drawing was not just to produce a record (because such a drawing could have been taken from a book), but as an exploratory activity using observation, both with the naked eye and magnifiers such as a hand lens and microscope. The task acted as a stimulus to further enquiry because as they were drawing, students raised many questions about the functions of the different parts, about similarities and differences between this and other creatures such as locusts which they had studied previously, about the type of life cycle and relative sizes of different crayfish. The act of drawing had provided a simple form of interaction between the students and the crayfish and had generated the sorts of questions we associate with a curious scientist. Subsequent teaching could now quite genuinely start from the questions raised by the students. Many of the questions could be researched from books as well as answered by the teacher.

Lesson 3 A-level biology lesson: study of crayfish: observation practical work

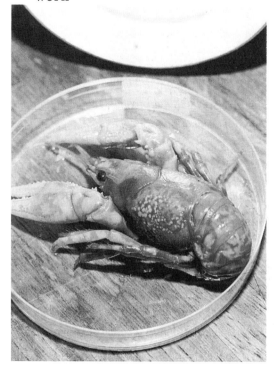

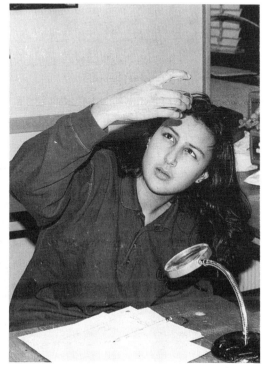

Plate 3.33 Preserved crayfish   Plate 3.34 Examining details of the crayfish

Lesson 3   A-level biology lesson: study of crayfish: observation practical work (cont.)

Plate 3.35 Drawing the crayfish

Plate 3.36 Linking features in book drawings to what can be seen on the specimen

Plate 3.37 Practical exploration and follow-up from books

Summary of the lessons

Well prepared and clearly defined tasks were key features of the lessons and allowed teachers to plan in detail and have everything that was needed ready in advance. Good organisation automatically freed the teacher to talk with students about the science involved, respond to individual needs and not waste unnecessary time on repeating or explaining organisational instructions. The purposes of the lessons were made explicit at the start, and time was set aside at the end to return to this. Thoughts were shared, ideas pulled together and the scene set for moving on to the next stage.

The distinction drawn between the types of practical work are not 'water-tight'. There is inevitably overlap. The lesson on recording temperature changes as water cools, while designed to develop practical skills, is also about the phenomenon of cooling. The lesson on fire, while designed to give understanding of fire-fighting, was also about students' practical skills to handle fire safely. The lesson on crayfish draws on the ability to observe detail and generate questions but also provides an opportunity for further practice of practical skills such as those involved in using a microscope. Similar overlaps can be seen in the next chapter on investigations.

Observation, perception and understanding

It would be a mistake not to include in this chapter the link between observation and understanding, because what is observed depends as much on what is in the mind of the observer as on what is there to be seen. It is yet another factor in the complex task of learning from practical work and has considerable bearings on the strategies a teacher must use.

One example from a science lesson and one from an everyday experience will suffice to illustrate the point. In a science lesson two students were observing what happened when they blew between two apples suspended on strings. They recorded that the apples moved apart. The teacher nearby noted this and asked them to check; again they agreed they moved apart; they were observing what they expected to happen. Only when the teacher insisted they watched again did they notice that the apples moved towards each other. Suddenly the unexpectedness of the phenomenon registered and they tried it several more times to find, quite rightly, that on every occasion the apples moved inwards towards each other.

The everyday example concerns the movement of the sun. 'The sun rises in the East and sets in the West' is commonly believed by people in the UK. Once it is pointed out that this occurs on only two days a year at the equinoxes, that in summer the sun rises increasingly towards the NE and sets towards NW and that in winter it rises S of E and sets S of W, people usually realise the significance of the sun coming into their buildings from different directions at different times of the year.

Abercrombie, in her book *The Anatomy of Judgement,* explored this aspect of observation from the standpoint of a teacher. She taught medical students and was concerned to improve their ability to interpret X-ray photographs. She they recorded individually what they observed and then shared their lists with each other. The total number of observations increased as different people saw different things. Disagreements about observations usually reflected different interpretations and forced the group to return to the photographs in order to look for further supporting evidence. Students learned the value of regarding observations and interpretations as tentative, of going back to evidence to check detail and of using other people as sounding boards. Discussion played an enormous part in increasing the reliability of observation.

It is worth returning to the three lessons described earlier in this chapter and studying the teachers' strategies in the light of this discussion on observation. In all of them we see the virtue in tight organisation so that teachers are free to listen to what students say and to talk with them about their observations. The first teacher asked students to predict what would happen; he did not ask just one child but several; he expected students to listen to one another and to comment if they disagreed. The second teacher discussed the theory of the fire triangle first, so that a relevant set of ideas were implanted before observations were made. In the third lesson individuals had time to observe, question, go to books for more information and then re-observe; as knowledge built up so did the scope and detail of their observations.

In practical work a further complication to observation is that apparatus often masks the phenomenon. The size and noise of the Van der Graaf generator often masks the significance of the spark being generated. The noise from the vacuum cleaner in a linear air track can distract from the significance of the movements of the air-borne pucks. People's memories of their school science often relate more to the dramatic equipment than to its significance for scientific ideas. Because of this a teacher may often be heard taking some time to explain a piece of apparatus, with the purpose of making it sufficiently familiar that the class can forget it and focus attention on the phenomenon.

The link between practical work and learning scientific theory

It is often believed that practical work is a key means of learning scientific theory. When Woolnough and Allsop, however, proposed categorising practical work into exercises, experiences and investigations, they had already argued that it was impossible to expect students to learn about scientific theories, laws and principles through direct experience in the laboratory. They argued that both 'cookbook' science of doing experiments to prove a scientific fact or principle, and 'guided heurism' to enable students to discover scientific theories were inappropriate uses of practical work.

'Cookbook' science dominated in schools in the early part of this century, and can be characterised as practical work designed to allow students to arrive, fairly straightforwardly, at the 'right answer'. Examples would include following instructions about bleaching and boiling leaves, some of which had been left in the dark, to 'prove' that starch is made in leaves, or breathing on a cold surface to 'prove' that there is water in breath. Such practical left no scope for students to design their own investigations, or to decide what observations might be relevant, or to discuss and negotiate meaning. It also implied that one might be relevant, or to discuss and negotiate meaning. It also implied that one piece of evidence was sufficient in science. What seemed to be ignored was that a range of theoretical arguments was needed to link the appearance of the liquid droplets on the cold surface with invisible water vapour; as was the fact that learners are often unconvinced by such explanations because they can think of others which at first seem equally plausible.

The word 'prove' has overtones of complete certainty which might be appropriate for Euclidean geometry but not for science. One practical never proved anything: neither in the development of science nor in the learning of science. A metal ball, when heated in the 'ball and ring' experiment, not going through the ring is consistent with the metal ball expanding because of the heat; but this explanation may not register with students because this phenomenon is also consistent with the ball swelling from absorbing the gas from the Bunsen burner. A greater experience than watching one experiment is needed to recognise that the first explanation is more reasonable than the second.

'Guided heurism' was expounded originally by Armstrong at the end of the last century. It aimed to put the pupil in the role of 'being a scientist'. The inclusion of practical work was justified on the grounds that science was inductive; i.e. that theories and generalisations came directly from observations. 'Guided' meant that the teacher created situations which allowed students to 'induce' the patterns, laws, etc. This tradition continued through to the 1960s when it was revisited with strength in the Nuffield O-level projects (Jenkins, 1979). It hung uncomfortably with the projects' view of science as requiring hypothetical deductive reasoning and with its explicit teaching of such imaginative leaps as Newton's in his development of the theories of gravitation.

Within both these traditions, 'cookbook' science and guided heurism, is an assumption that practical experience automatically speaks to the observer with one unequivocal message. The experience of any thoughtful science teacher is that this is not the case. The reason lies in the nature of scientific theory, which essentially goes beyond perceptual experience. It represents the models we have of how the natural world works. These models must be consistent with observations, but inevitably incorporate features which cannot be seen and have to be imagined. Imagination had to be used by the scientists who dreamed them up in the first place, and has to be used by those who come afterwards and want to understand the models. It was arguments like these which Woolnough and Allsop used when they suggested that on many occasions it would make more sense to separate the teaching of theories from practical work:

> We believe that the common notion that practical work is used primarily to discover, or to aid understanding of, the theoretical content of accepted science must be changed. The two aspects of science, the content and the process, have become inextricably mixed in our science teaching. We believe that a beginning should be made by releasing practical from the shackles of theory, and attending to process as a separate objective important in its own right. We will make no progress until we have cut this Gordian knot. (Woolnough and Allsop, 1985, pp. 39–40)

Lesson 4   A-Level Physics lesson on the wave theory of light

Plate 3.38 Using diffraction gratings

Plate 3.39 Studying photographs of diffraction patterns in a book

Lesson 4   A-Level Physics lesson on the wave theory of light (cont.)

Plate 3.40 Listening to the teacher's theoretical explanation

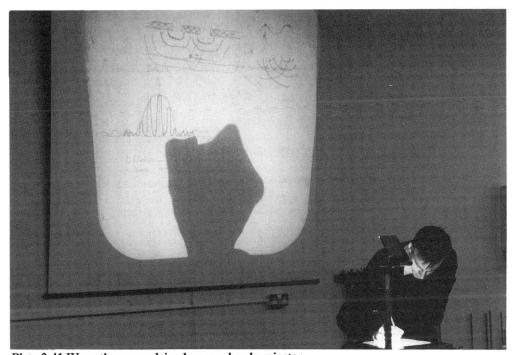

Plate 3.41 Wave theory explained on overhead projector

Lesson 4 A-Level Physics: a non-practical lesson

A lesson we photographed illustrated this well (plates 3.38–3.41). It was an A-level physics lesson on the wave explanation of effects produced when light is passed through narrow slits. Once or twice the teacher reminded the group of the phenomenon (plate 3.38); he also referred to pictures of interference and diffraction patterns in water waves (plate 3.39); but much of his time was spent in exposition, explaining how the wave model of light was consistent with the phenomenon (plates 3.40, 3.41). Dialogue between class and teacher formed part of the lesson as did application of ideas to problems. Essentially the means by which this group came to understand the theory was *not* practical in nature, because the explanations are essentially abstract. This is a feature of much science.

Tamir (1991) pointed out that this occurred particularly in physics and chemistry. In chemistry an experimenter 'observes colours, temperatures, smells, hears explosions...and explains them in terms of atoms, molecules, electrovalent and covalent bonds...which cannot be seen but form the conceptual basis for explanation'. In physics 'work with electric circuits is explained in terms of electrons.... waves, momentum, force, energy and pressure are other concepts in physics'. There are, however, examples from other fields of science, such as ecology, biology, geology, astronomy, which require abstract explanation. No science teacher is exempt from the responsibility of taking students into the world of the imagination.

The interplay between theoretical understanding and practical experience must not be ignored, however. In the physics lesson above the teacher explained how the wave theory was consistent with the observation of diffraction patterns and reminded students of the observations. The interplay also affects a person's approach to practical activities and this is particularly apparent in those where students have to decide how to proceed, as in the investigations which are the subject of Chapter 4.

References

DES (1991) *National Curriculum in Technology*, London: HMSO

Foulds, K., Gott, R. and Feasey, R. (1992) *Investigative Work in Science, A Report by the Exploration of Science Team to the National Curriculum Council*, University of Durham

Gott, R. and Foulds, K. (1989) *The Assessment of Practical Work*, London: Blackwell

Jenkins, E.W. (1979) *From Armstrong to Nuffield*, London: John Murray

Johnson Abercrombie, M. L. (1960) *The Anatomy of Judgement*, London: Pelican

NCC (1989) *Non Statutory Guidance* (to Science in the National Curriculum): *Section D: Exploration in Science*, London: HMSO

NCC (1993) *Teaching Science at Key Stages 3 and 4*, York: NCC

Tamir (1991) 'Practical Work in school science: an analysis of current practice' in Woolnough (ed.) (1991), pp. 13–20

Woolnough, B. (ed.) (1991) *Practical Science: The role and reality of practical work in school science*, Lewes: Falmer Press

Woolnough, B. and Allsop, T. (1985) *Practical Work in Science*, Cambridge: Cambridge University Press

Further Reading

APU (1990) *Assessment Matters No. 8: Observation in School Science*, London: SEAC

Buchan, A.S. 'Practical Assessment in GCSE science. The diversity of the examination group practices', *School Science Review*, June 1992, 73 (265), pp.19–28.

Gee, B. and Glackson, S. G. 'The origin of practical work in the English school science curriculum', *School Science Review*, June 1992, 73 (265), pp.79–83.

Hodson, D. 'A critical look at practical work in school science', *School Science Review*, March 1990, 70 (256), pp. 33–9

Hodson, D. 'Redefining and reorienting practical work in school science', *School Science Review*, March 1992, 73 (264), pp.65–78

Osborne, J. (1993) 'Alternatives to practical work', *School Science Review*, 75 (271) pp.117–123

Strang, J. (1990) *Assessment Matters No. 1: Measurement in School Science*, London: SEAC

Taylor, R.M. and Swatton, P. (1990) *Assessment Matters No. 1: Graph Work in School Science*, London: SEAC

Wellington, J. (ed.) (1989) *Skills and Processes in Science Education*, London: Routledge.

4
SCIENTIFIC INVESTIGATIONS AND TECHNOLOGICAL TASKS
Jenny Frost

Introduction

'Investigations', the category of practical work not dealt with in Chapter 3, form the subject of this chapter. In order to explore teachers' roles in managing these, they have been subdivided into 'scientific investigations', which typically require students to design an experiment to find something out, and 'technological tasks' which typically require students to design and make some artefact. Such work is usually open-ended so that students have to make decisions for themselves and learn that there may be several equally valid ways of proceeding. The variety of activities that teachers can create to make this possible will emerge as the chapter progresses, but two important common threads run through them all. They both relate to the role of the teacher. First, in all the situations described it is essential for teachers to give students opportunities to think for themselves, make mistakes, and modify ideas. Second, creating and organising the settings in which these activities can occur are keys to success but require considerable expertise on the part of the teacher.

These two aspects of a teacher's job can be seen in examples of open-ended activities elsewhere in the book. In Chapter 8, the teacher who asked students to design an organism which is adapted to a particular environment, or the teacher in Chapter 2 who provided the challenge of making a one-minute thiosulphate clock, provided the setting and resources in which students created their own answers to the problems. The water fluoridation debate in Chapter 7 is another open-ended activity of a different kind where students had to select appropriate information in order to create an argument and support their case. The teacher created the setting and climate in which this could occur and recognised the importance of standing back and allowing the students to develop their own thinking through debate.

Nature of scientific investigations and technological tasks

The use of scientific investigations in school derives from notions of 'being a scientist for a day' and the use of technological tasks and problems from 'being a technologist for a day'. Hence much of the literature about these involves analysis of what scientists and technologists do, and the contexts in which they work. This is not the place to examine the debates about the nature of science and technology; but it is possible to illustrate some differences by an anecdote told by a technology consultant in his talks 'What is technology?' (given to beginning teachers at the London Institute of Education in the early 1980s). Early in his career he undertook research into thermodynamics at university and published papers on what he had found out. He was later employed by NASA to help with a problem with one of their rockets, which had a tendency to fall back to earth when it was not supposed to. When he and collaborators finally resolved the problem, having drawn on past knowledge of thermodynamics and new findings generated during the task, he asked where he might publish; to which the answer was 'Publish? The rocket stayed up. What more do you want?'

Here we see one of the contrasts often cited: the purpose of science being to add to a store of knowledge; the purpose of technology being to get a particular job done. It is possible to see this contrast in the problems posed in schools. 'Design an experiment to find the factors which affect viscosity of a liquid' at the science end; 'Find a liquid which maintains constant viscosity over a temperature range of 5–50° C' at the technology end.

Both scientific and technological tasks are incorporated in the same chapter because the similarities outweigh the differences. If students engaged in these are watched, there will be times when in some respects it is impossible to distinguish between the two. Similar skills and processes are involved, namely, deciding how to go about the task, deciding which materials and instruments to use, working with apparatus and equipment, collecting data, deciding how many times measurements have to be repeated, recording results, making interpretations. Both require patience and commitment to the task.

Teachers also find considerable overlap in the planning and management of the two types of tasks. In both cases they have to think about whether to provide limited resources so that students have to work within specified constraints, or whether to impose the need to select from a wide range of resources; whether to ask students to undertake the initial planning away from apparatus, because the decision alters significantly the task for the student. Teachers also have to encourage students to generate their own ideas and yet know when and how to intervene if, say, one group is becoming particularly frustrated with slow progress.

Obviously differences should not be ignored. The different purposes manifest themselves particularly at the appraisal stage. In the scientific task appraisal involves reflecting on the methods used to collect data, the scope and validity of the data, the reliability of interpretations. In the technological task the appraisal involves testing the product to see to what extent it fulfils the criteria set up at the start.

Returning again to the work of career scientists or technologists, the purpose of their work is in most cases apparent to them. They may be members of a community of scientists in a university, who are collectively exploring an area of common interest and research. They may be part of a team studying problems for the Medical Research Council; or consultants to Friends of the Earth, monitoring environmental changes and influences; or in a research lab in industry, improving and developing new techniques. There will be a few lone scientists pursuing their own line of research. Whatever the setting, as individuals, they will have some rationale for devoting many hours to this enterprise.

The question of context and purpose is also important for students in school. The context must be sufficiently meaningful to them in some way to engage their intellectual curiosity. There is evidence that this engagement is likely to be enhanced if the students themselves can be involved in the generation of the problem. It is possible to illustrate what a teacher might do to create a meaningful context by recourse to one example. Suppose a teacher sets a problem, 'Find what proportion of leaves on a tree are damaged', there is no reason why this, on its own, should provide sufficient motivation for the completion of what can be a tedious exercise. It may surprise the reader to imagine that anyone would, but recent emphasis on process science has led, in a few cases, to disjointed activities in totally unrelated contexts. For this particular activity it is possible to imagine a teacher introducing it within the context of ecology and ecological pyramids; trying to gain some quantitative estimate of the weight of plant material necessary to maintain the herbivore population which in turn supports the first layer of carnivores and so on. In fact it may have been presented in the form of 'How could we find out how much plant material is needed to support this pyramid?'. The teacher may also discuss the task in terms of scientific procedures, inviting students to consider problems of sampling, of acquiring reliable data, of deciding how to measure, of putting the results from different experimenters together.

This preparation of context is not just a question of motivation and purpose. To be able to undertake a systematic investigation it is necessary to understand quite a lot about the phenomenon first, otherwise the experimenter has no chance to think about possible ways of proceeding. Even for adult scientists or technologists this is important. When they meet a new phenomenon they engage in an initial exploratory phase, learning something about the parameters of the task in front of them. A teacher must also recognise the importance of such an introductory phase and for this purpose use mostly observation and illustrative practical work. The introductory, exploratory phase, of course, does not suddenly cease and the investigation start. There is a slow transition between the two, and this accounts for the continual need for modifications experienced by any investigator.

Examples of investigations and technological tasks

The increased interest in using investigations has led to a slow accumulation of examples that are appropriate within the time, resources and curriculum constraints in schools, but generating examples has proved more challenging than expected (Jennings, 1992, Watts and West, 1992). Teachers' guidance for examination syllabuses, science text books which have adopted a 'process approach' to learning science (for example, Screen, 1986), guidance for the National Curriculum, are all useful sources along with accounts from teachers and lecturers such as appear in the ASE's publication, *School Science Review*. A short list of resources is given at the end of the chapter.

Examples available show that scientific investigations typically involve students in finding factors which affect phenomena, comparing performances of materials and gadgets, quantifying or coding phenomena, or collecting evidence to support a hypothesis or prediction. Technological tasks typically involve students in making a phenomenon happen within specified constraints; making an artefact to meet certain criteria; evaluating and adapting an existing design or technique; modelling a system; or taking an established industrial technique and trying it out on a laboratory scale.

Scientific investigations: examples

a) Finding factors which affect a phenomenon

These require students to predict the likely factors and find ways of collecting data to examine the effect of one or more factor. This usually involves controlling as best as possible all variables except the one being investigated. A small number are given in the box below.

Find the factors which affect:

    the viscosity of glycerol;
    the rate of dissolving of water purifying tablets;
    the loss of water from plants;
    the rate of heart beat of daphnia;
    the weathering of limestone;
    the rate of descent of a parachute, etc.

Investigations, expressed in this way, require students first to predict possible factors or combination of factors. If, then, they give reasons for their predictions, they are hypothesising about principles governing the phenomenon.

Alternatively the factors may be specified and the student asked to investigate how a phenomenon is affected by them, as shown in the box below.

Factors specified: how they affect the phenomenon to be investigated

    Is the rate of dissolving of water purifying tablets affected by crushing the tablet or by using hot/cold water;
    Is the strength of hair affected by whether it is washed or unwashed?;
    What is the relationship between the size of a spark gap and voltage?;
    What is the effect of different plant spacing on plant growth?

In many ecological situations questions would be phrased differently because controlling variables is difficult and the possible variables are complex. Plant and animal populations are therefore frequently monitored and patterns sought in the data. Eventually possible reasons for the patterns are considered as a means of identifying significant factors. A salutary story can illustrate the technique and some of the problems. A group of biology undergraduates were set the task of recording the plant species on a particular field. The field was divided up and students took responsibility for different sections. Data was analysed by a computer programme designed to search for patterns of distribution for which the group then sought possible explanations. There was one pattern which defied explanation: the number and variety of species was much less on one side than the other, and this could not be accounted for in terms of light levels, soil types, drainage variations, previous sowing or fertilising regimes. It was only when someone spotted that first-year undergraduates collected the data on the side with fewer species and third-year undergraduates on the other side, that the relevant variable was identified. In teaching this possibility cannot be ignored.

b) Quantifying a particular phenomenon

There are many cases in science when moving from a qualitative to a quantitative description creates a deeper understanding and these can be used in school science.

Devise a way to:

  measure the variation of water flow in a river;
  explore the extent of leaf damage;
  investigate the extent of weathering and estimate when the building will be completely weathered away;
  monitor the variation in pond population over a period of 2 months.

---

c) Comparing performances of materials and gadgets

These are the problems that have parallels with those from a testing department in industry or the research labs of a consumer association and have earned themselves the name 'Which?-type' tests after the consumer magazine of that name. They involve devising an experiment to compare several products for a specific property, as shown in the box below. Some are presented in a consumer-type context where the price of the product is specified and the students are asked to evaluate the best buy.

Compare the:
  absorbing qualities of different nappies;
  performance of different fertilisers;
  strengths of different sticky tapes;
  insulating properties of different materials.

These tests tend to be most productive, scientifically, if they are followed by a consideration of the factors that make one product better than another. This takes students' thinking into hypothesizing about significant factors and into considering how to collect further evidence for their hypotheses.

d) Testing a hypothesis

Examples have been mentioned already in the categories above. Others can be found in the literature on children's alternative frameworks. An example is given in Osborne and Freyberg (1985). Students in a class believed that when water turned into steam it had changed into separate gaseous components, hydrogen and oxygen. The teacher invited the students to predict what would happen if she put a match to steam if this were the case (the students already knew the effect of burning hydrogen in air). The class devised an experiment to test their ideas and of course found the steam did not explode.

Technological problems: examples

e) Making a phenomenon happen within specified constraints

These come in the form of a challenge to control a phenomenon in some way.

> For example:
>   'Make a one-minute timer';
>   'Make a circuit which will ring a bell when it begins to rain';
>   'Grow the biggest potato'.

As with the scientific investigations of 'finding a factor...', these problems require students to predict what factors might help them achieve their goal and test them out by trial and error.

f) Designing and making an artefact to meet certain criteria

> Examples of this are:
>   Make a boat that will carry a load of so much, the boat must travel in a straight line;
>   Make a toy that has moving parts and will appeal to children between 5 and 10;
>   Design and make a sundial that works, is robust enough to leave outside and can be taken home;
>   Design and build an anemometer, locate it in a suitable place outside and take a series of readings. Can you connect the anemometer to a computer for automatic monitoring?

It is easy to adapt these to have a commercial component; students can be asked to cost the enterprise; they might even be asked to undertake selling if the product is worthy of it. Again these tasks require an understanding of possible features to alter to achieve the required goal.

g) Modelling a system

A problem in this category would be 'Make a model of the human thorax to show the action of the diaphragm in breathing'. There is a standard model described in many textbooks which uses a bell jar to represent the rib cage and balloons to represent the lungs. If, however, groups have to make their own models they have to put their existing knowledge into practice. When we set this to a group once, they replaced the bell jar with half a clear plastic drinks bottle. This had the advantage that it reduced the space between the balloons (lungs) and bottle (rib cage) which is a major drawback of the usual model. However, the bottle, being made of plastic and not glass, caved in under the increased tension as the rubber diaphragm was pulled down. Not until this happened did the group understand the significance of a rigid rib cage and consider the forces it must have to withstand.

h) Evaluating and adapting an existing design or technique

Two examples of this type are:
    Design and make a simple, portable solar cooker. Consider how efficient the device is in: collecting solar energy, storing energy, keeping a consistent temperature;
    Evaluate the reliablity and sensistivity of a new measuring device

i) Adapting an established industrial technique and trying it out on a laboratory scale

Two examples of this type are:
    Making paper and testing the properties of it;
    The extraction of antibiotics from lichens.

This type is being developed further by the chemical industry education centre at the University of York in their series *Making use of science and technology* (1993).

    Technological tasks have proved to be useful vehicles for learning new information and understanding. From the few examples given here it is evident that students will frequently have to look up technical information in order to proceed or will face scientific principles as their models and artefacts do not necessarily perform in the way they expected. One further example to illustrate this comes from the boat making task in f) above. Students often produce models of a 'self-propelling sail boat' with air from a balloon mounted on the boat blowing directly into a sail at the other end of the boat, only to find that the boat does not move. It usually does not take long for the groups to spot that the jet propulsion from the balloon balances the force of the expelled air on the sail.
    The nature of a task is of course altered by whether it is selected by the teacher and presented to the class, or whether it is generated by the students. The extent to which resources and techniques are supplied also affects the demands made on students. Because the mode of presentation can have a significant effect, Watts and Bentley (1992) found it useful to distinguish GIVEN problems (where the solvers are given the goal and the strategy) from GOAL problems (where the solvers are given the goal and nothing else; they have to decide and develop their own strategies) and OWN problems where solvers decide both the goal and the strategies.

The majority found in school are 'goal' and 'given'. They have the advantage that a teacher can plan ahead in order to match the task to particular curriculum content and hence can keep a tighter control over the learning. It also restricts the number of activities that might be going on in a class at any one time. They have the disadvantage that they may not be so motivating for students who lack initial ownership of the problem. The examples we photographed for this chapter came into the category of goal problems.

Phases of investigations and problems

Figure 4.1 gives the stages of investigations as described by APU, the Assessment of Performance Unit, and those drawn up for guidance by the Nuffield A-level Biology project.

APU	Nuffield A level Biology
1a. Problem perception	• Identification and selection of a problem
1b. Problem reformulation	• Legal and ethical considerations
2. Planning	• Investigation of available knowledge
3. Carrying out the experiment	• Designing the investigation
4. Recording the data	• Carrying out the practical work
5. Interpreting data	• Assembly and presentation of results
and drawing conclusions	• Drawing inferences
6a. Evaluation of results	• Relating inferences to background
6b. Evaluation of method	knowledge and suggestions for further
	investigations
	• Bibliography and acknowledgements

Figure 4.1 Stages in investigations: APU and Nuffield A-level Biology compared

The APU list was devised specifically for analysing the performance of students aged 11, 13 and 15 years on 'given' problems which could be completed in about 40 minutes. The Nuffield A-level booklet was written for academically able students, often in the age group 16–19 years, embarking on long-term projects in which they are expected to identify their own problem, undertake the necessary background reading and set their results in the context of the reading. Similar descriptions can be seen in the three 'strands' of investigating used in *NC Science* (see pp.174–5).

While these descriptions can provide a useful guide to both student and teacher they can be misleading because they can imply a linear progression from one stage to the next. Investigators rarely go systematically through the stages from start to finish without returning to 'earlier' stages. They plan and replan as they go along; they refocus the problem; they find data collected at the start signals the need to modify procedures, etc.

Attempts to represent this oscillation to and fro between phases in diagrammatic form generally replace a linear list by a cyclical one, as in the representation, produced by APU, shown in Figure 4.2. APU point out that there is continual feedback from one stage to earlier ones and that it would be appropriate to draw far more return lines on the drawing.

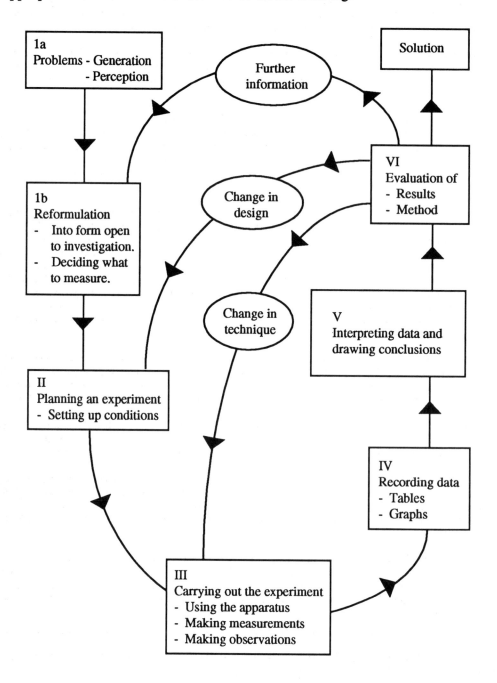

Figure 4.2 Investigations: cycle of events, APU

1a PROBLEM PERCEPTION Here students decide what the question means and what it is asking them to do. In this case one would expect something like 'Do I blink as fast when I am reading as when I am running?'. 'Does the same thing happen for another person?'. Recognising that the problem is susceptible to investigation is important as APU found some students answering questions from background knowledge, not realising they should collect first-hand information.

1b PROBLEM REFORMULATION Having identified variables, students have to decide what to vary, what to measure and what to control; in this case *the number of blinks in a given time* is the variable to be measured; *the activity*, the variable to be changed; and *the person and general conditions*, the variables to be kept constant.

2 PLANNING This involves deciding what apparatus is needed, what recording is to be done, and how many measurements will have to be made. Students will have to decide what 'activities' they will use, how many different activities, for how long they should time them, whether they should count the number of blinks in a minute or whether to time ten blinks, how to extend the study to include more than one person. They must have some idea how these measurements will help them answer the question.

3 CARRYING OUT THE EXPERIMENT They have to make a choice of the appropriate measuring instrument and develop and carry out a measuring strategy as accurately as possible. This may involve deciding how many people are needed to carry out the investigation. It is very often at this stage that students effectively do a trial run and have to rethink their plans. They discover that a blink is not always easy to identify – when is a movement only a twitch? An operational definition of some sort has to be created. If the subject happens to have an exceptionally low blink rate the time scale over which measurements are being made may have to be extended. They may decide to work in threes. There may be several trial and error phases before the planning is sufficiently refined to proceed. Once the procedure is organised, the actual measurements can take a long time; boredom may set in and with it sloppy measurements.

4 RECORDING THE DATA This can be in a variety of forms; for this particular investigation a table would be appropriate. Decisions on how to record should be made at the planning stage; this helps students to clarify their planning. Again, however, when they start to record they sometimes have to modify the table because of inappropriate number of columns.

5 INTERPRETING DATA AND DRAWING CONCLUSION To some extent students interpret data as they collect it and this often prompts the need to take more measurements or to check one or two readings. But on the whole this is not tackled well without the intervention of the teacher.

6a EVALUATION OF RESULTS This requires students to go back to the original question and give an answer consistent with the evidence collected. This stage again sometimes forces students back to an earlier stage. For instance, they may not have extended the investigation to a second or even third person, so they will not know whether the change in the blink rate of one subject is similar to that of another.

6b EVALUATION OF THE METHOD This requires students to look critically at the methods and acknowledge the limitations. For instance, the people counting the blinks will never know whether a blink was missed because they blinked. Such limitations are inherent in the experiment and are difficult to eliminate. Often the teacher will have set a constraint on time and this limits the number of observations that can be made.

Figure 4.3 Description of APU stages for a simple investigation into whether the rate of blinking is affected by the activity a person is doing.

Figure 4.3 is another attempt to illustrate what happens at different stages (using the APU list) in terms of a fairly simple investigation on finding out whether people's blink-rates are affected by the activity that they are doing.

There are similar, but not identical, stages in technological tasks. They comprise a problem perception/selection/identification stage, followed by consideration of the constraints such as time, resources, expertise, then comes the generation of possible solutions, selection of a solution, carrying out the solution and eventually evaluating the final product in terms of the initial task. Again, a cyclical representation with feedback lines from one stage to another matches the way in which people tackle tasks. The diagram in Figure 4.4 adapted from one which appears in the *County of Avon Resources* (1983) is typical of pictorial descriptions of a technological problem-solving cycle.

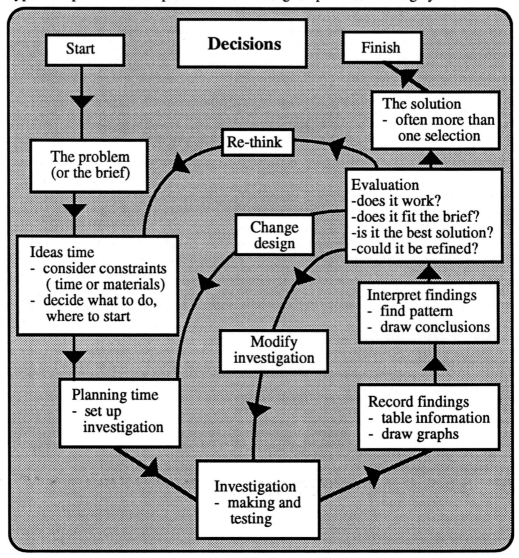

Figure 4.4 Technological tasks: cycle of events (source: *County of Avon Resources*, 1983)

Management of scientific investigations

An understanding of these stages from the investigator's point of view is crucial for teachers if they are to manage these situations and ensure they are effective learning experiences for the students.

The descriptions above indicate that there is thinking to be done and decisions to be made during investigations. Teachers' skills lie in their ability to enable students to undertake the thinking and decision making for themselves. It is all too easy for a teacher to take over and tell students what to do, or at the other extreme leave them too much at sea, with insufficient guidance because of a concern to make students think for themselves. After a while teachers build up a repertoire of useful question and comments to support students, such as 'Have you decided what to measure/ how to measure/ how to record...?'; 'Don't forget you have to decide...'; 'How will that provide you with the evidence that you need?'; 'Look at the table of results, what are significant trends?', etc.

Roles teachers take in these investigations must complement and support the roles of students. The nature of this support is explored in the series of photographs we took of three different teachers as they involved students in investigations and technological tasks.

Lesson 1 Planning an investigation: yoghurt production

In plates 4.1 to 4.4 the teacher set aside a lesson for students to plan how they would investigate the factors which affect the production of yoghurt. By the end of the lesson plans of procedures and apparatus lists had to be submitted in written form. The students worked in small groups sharing ideas and refining plans. The teacher had anticipated the difficulties associated with the problem perception stage and had asked the students to read the investigation through to each other at the start and spent a few minutes ensuring that it was understood. Once this was done the groups worked on their own (plate 4.1). As plans developed and were committed to paper the teacher invited groups to explain what they intended to do and to give their reasons. The discussions helped to clarify ideas and procedures. The teacher did not passively accept the students' ideas; he negotiated and helped to improve plans.

By the end of the lesson, the plans were sufficiently detailed for students to write out their requests for equipment that they would need in order to undertake the investigation the following lesson.

Lesson 1 Planning an investigation

Plate 4.1 Joint planning; sharing ideas

Plate 4.2 Teacher listening to plans

Lesson 1 Planning an investigation (cont.)

Plate 4.3 Teacher pondering on plans

Plate 4.4 Students explaining plans to the teacher

Lesson 2 Putting an experimental plan into action

Plate 4.5 Reminding the class of the questions set

Plate 4.6 Indicating the apparatus that the class had ordered

Plate 4.7 Collecting soil and water (science was in a classroom without water supply)

Lesson 2 Putting an experimental plan into action (cont.)

Plate 4.8 An uncertain start – a characteristic stage in investigations

Plate 4.9 Investigations well under way with systematic measurements being made

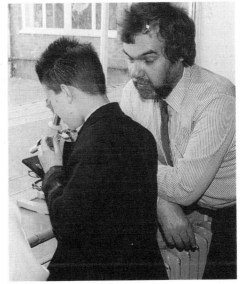

Plate 4.10 Discussing whether a microscope is a useful tool for the investigation

Lesson 2 Putting an experimental plan into action: soils

The next series of photographs (plates 4.5–4.10) shows a class at the subsequent stage of carrying out experiments, but on a different investigation. Students had already planned how they would go about the investigation and had ordered necessary equipment. The questions posed were:

> Which of three soils allows water to go through quickest?
> Which of these three soils holds water most?
> How much soil is water?
> How much soil is air?

The teacher reminded the class of the questions (plate 4.5) and explained that all the apparatus that was requested had been supplied (plate 4.6). He made no comment on whether he thought their choice was appropriate or not. Once the students began their investigations, they paused for thought and modified their plans. There was a sense of an untidy phase to the lesson, but the teacher deliberately did not interfere, allowing students to sort out their own ideas. Before long most were under way (plate 4.9).

An interesting phenomenon began to occur. One or two students had ordered thermometers and microscopes, even though these were not needed. Often when inappropriate apparatus is ordered students soon realise for themselves that they do not need it. On this occasion this did not happen (plate 4.10) and soon over half the class began to ask for these pieces of equipment, anxious probably that they had forgotten something. The event was useful because it allowed the teacher to recognise that there was still a lot of thinking that needed refining. At this point the whole class was stopped for a short time while he discussed whether they really needed these pieces of equipment. They soon identified with his help that they were unnecessary. It is this ability to judge when an intervention is appropriate which lies so much at the heart of the art of good teaching.

The follow-up to this lesson involved the collection of results, discussion of discrepancies between one group's findings and another, interpretation of results, consideration of the methods used and finally a brief discussion on the problems of being an investigator. In other words, the teacher took them through the interpretation of data, evaluation of results, and the evaluation of methods stages noted in the APU list. It is important that the teacher does take a more prominent role at these later stages, because students do not spontaneously recognise the importance of them.

Management of technological tasks

There are similarities between the management of technological tasks and the management of scientific investigations. There are similar needs to clarify and focus the problem and to generate ideas; to use teacher and peers as a sounding board; and for the teacher not to interfere too much and to note points that should be brought out in the summary at the end.

Lessons 3a, 3b, 3c Undertaking a technological task

To illustrate this we followed the first three lessons of a series of four, devoted to a technological task. The task set was to devise a means of dropping an egg from a height of three metres onto the tarmac without breaking the egg. This was a 'goal' problem, with the time, resources and challenge made available, but requiring the class to decide how to proceed. The class (Y9, i.e. 13–14-year-olds) were sufficiently intrigued to have a go even though there was no obvious need for dropping eggs.

Time management

The three lessons covered developing ideas, drawing up plans, making devices and testing them (plates 4.11–4.35). The fourth, which was not photographed, covered discussion of what had been learned and the relevance to 'real' problems. As with all teaching, organisation of time is critical; an apparently seamless task has to be divided into time slots of just over an hour so that a class can easily pick up from the end of a lesson at the start of the next, one or two days later. Something tangible has to remain to act as a reminder for the next lesson. The first lesson, lesson 3a, was divided into two main sections: brainstorming with the teacher (plates 4.11–4.14) followed by the class developing initial ideas in small groups (plates 4.15–4.18). By the end of the lesson groups had some ideas on paper. In lesson 3b (plates 4.19–4.25) these were developed into detailed plans, showing particular design features and measurements which could be used as the blueprint for the making session in lesson 3c (plates 4.26–4.35). Testing of the devices took place in the latter part of lesson 3c (plates 4.31–4.35). Reports written for homework after lesson 3c formed the basis of discussion for the fourth lesson.

One difficult task was keeping the whole class on the same time-plan so that all models could be tested together at the end. There are no simple ways of doing this, but it is worth noting the strategies which this teacher used. First, the time plan was set and made explicit at the start. This was effective as everyone has the tendency to fill the time available; if time is short, corners are cut, decisions made which might otherwise be delayed and risks are taken of going ahead with less certainty of success than might be desired. Time reminders were important features of these lessons. Second, once the teacher had set groups working he was free to decide how best to divide his time to support different groups. The distribution of his time was not even. Third, this school had the policy of teaching mixed ability classes up to the end of Y9, hence the range of ability in any one class could be large with potential for creating time-management problems. The school supported this policy by appointing 'support teachers' who worked in classes where there were children with specific learning difficulties. Two support teachers supported this class on different days and the one in the first lesson is shown in plate 4.17. They worked mostly but not exclusively with groups which contained students who had been identified as in need of extra help and hence contributed to everyone keeping more or less to the same time-plan.

Space management

The teacher incorporated seven different types of activity into this series of lessons: whole class brainstorming; small group discussions; small group practical work; individuals writing and drawing by themselves; groups reporting to the whole class; exposition by the teacher to the whole class; the whole class watching the testing of the final products. Benches were fixed although stools could be moved. The different arrangements used can be seen from the photographs.

Teaching how to tackle the task

This was the first time that the class had worked with this teacher on such a task which meant that students did not automatically know how to go about it. Throughout the lessons there was considerable teaching on how to proceed; this comprised explaining what decisions had to be made, *but not making the decisions for the students*. For instance, the teacher used the brainstorming session in lesson 3a to show techniques for working in a group to generate and develop ideas. Ideas had to be put to the class as a whole; no discussion, however relevant, was allowed between people sitting next to each other because the whole group would not be able to participate. All ideas had to be entertained even if they at first sight seemed silly, because it was often apparently hare-brained ones which produced genuine innovations. People had to be patient and give others time to explain.

Briefing the class at the start

Each lesson started with a clear outline of what the teacher expected to be achieved in the time available. Plate 4.19 shows the start of the second lesson, 3b, with the teacher setting the task of completing plans in a written form ready to present to the class in the latter part of the lesson. He explained that the presentations (plates 4.23–4.25) allowed ideas to be shared with others who understood the task sufficiently to give useful feedback and provide critical questioning (plates 4.24, 4.25). Even though time constraints did not allow all groups to present their plans, the teacher explained that this was not necessary because considering other people's ideas helps listeners to reflect on their own and possibly make improvements.

There were numerous little ways in which the teacher's comments to, and interactions with, small groups reinforced the necessary way of working. Plate 4.20 captures him as a listener; plate 4.14 as a questioner; plate 4.29 as a provider of moral support or guidance to help meet deadlines. In plate 4.16 he appears as a silent catalyst to a discussion between two students and one senses that his presence may have been necessary although he appears to be doing nothing. Perhaps he provided the security that if the discussion led into areas that were not well understood he would intervene and help it forward.

Lesson 3a 'Brainstorming', the start of the technological task

Plate 4.11 Explaining procedures for a brainstorming session in a large group

Plate 4.12 Seating for whole class discussion in a laboratory with fixed benches

Lesson 3a   'Brainstorming', the start of the technological task (cont.)

Plate 4.13 The teacher explains that all ideas have to be directed to the whole group

Plate 4.14 Sharing ideas with the whole group

Lesson 3a Initial planning in a technological task (cont.)

Plate 4.15 Co-operative planning

Plate 4.16 The teacher as a silent catalyst?

Lesson 3a   Initial planning in a technological task (cont.)

Plate 4.17 Support teacher working with one group

Plate 4.18 Trial and error: exploration to help conceptualise the task

Lesson 3b Developing plans, committing them to paper

Plate 4.19 Teacher briefing the class before they start the second stage

Plate 4.20 The teacher listens to ideas

Lesson 3b Developing plans, committing them to paper (cont.)

Plate 4.21 The discussion continues

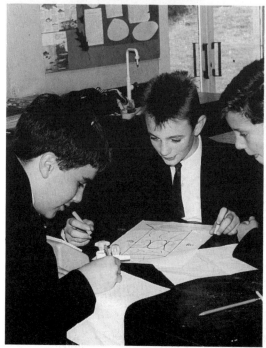

Plate 4.22 Plans are near completion

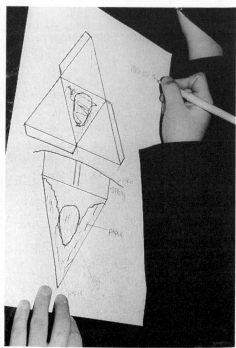

Plate 4.23 Plans ready for presentation

Lesson 3b Sharing plans with the rest of the class (cont.)

Plate 4.24 Plans: questions from the teacher

Plate 4.25 Plans: questions from the class

Lesson 3c   Making the models

Plate 4.26 The making starts

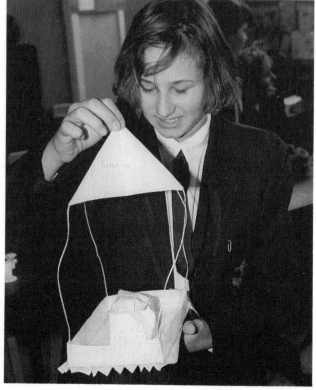

Plate 4.27 Nearly ready for testing

Lesson 3c   Making the models (cont.)

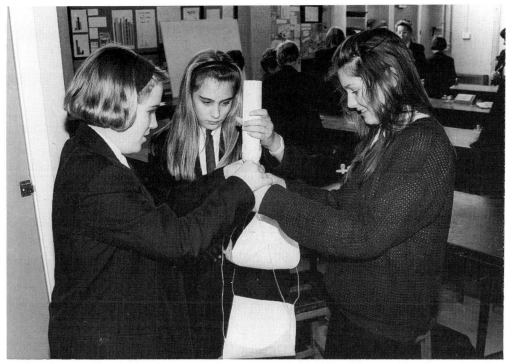

Plate 4.28 Mounting the cushioning device to go under the parachute

Plate 4.29 Last-minute work to complete on time

Lesson 3c   Making the models (cont.)

Plate 4.30 Testing a model

Plate 4.31 Examining for cracks

Lesson 3c (cont.) Testing the final product

Plate 4.32 Perfectly intact

Plate 4.33 Were all as successful? Examining the damage

Lesson 3c   Testing the final product (cont.)

Plate 4.34 It could have been much worse

Plate 4.35 Noting the homework

Development of ideas

During the brainstorming in lesson 3a, the idea of using a parachute to slow down the rate of fall coupled with a means of cushioning impact emerged. The cushioning devices were to be carried with the parachute. Sustaining a flow of ideas from students during brainstorming draws on a range of skills. This teacher used questions in several ways: to elicit greater detail from a student who had put forward an idea ('How big do you think you'll need your parachute?'); to suggest there might be a wider range of possible solutions ('How else could you ensure a safe landing?'); and to invite detail from the whole group ('You'll have to think of a way of attaching the egg; any ideas?'). He used extended pauses to allow ideas to be formulated. He spotted facial signs ('You seem to have an idea') even when students had not put up their hands to signal they had something to contribute. He rigidly maintained the climate necessary for sharing ideas by stopping one to one discussion immediately ('There will be time for one to one discussions in your small groups later.') and by listening to every idea that was put forward, and insisting the class did the same.

By the end of the brainstorming the task could have been considered solved because necessary features had been identified. Plates 4.15–4.18, however, show that more details still had to be settled: how big is an egg and how much does it weigh?; will the parachute hold it?; what is the best shape box?; what structures will take the impact?; what can be used to attach the parachute?; what do we use for sticking the paper?; how much sellotape is allowed?, etc. It became apparent that solving a problem in principle is never the same as doing it in practice. This phase drew quite extensively on students' existing knowledge of structures and parachutes; knowledge likely to have come almost entirely from everyday experience and therefore likely to be subconsciously learned. One of the impressive factors of tasks like this is that students often discover that they know facts without previously being aware that they knew them. In addition students also drew on simple exploration for a source of information (plate 4.18).

Plates 4.26–4.29 reveal that still further decisions were necessary as the students moved from their detailed plans to actual making. Some found modifications necessary. Each level presents a new task to tackle and has intrinsically its own form of open-endedness.

Mike Watts gives an interesting anecdote from a similar lesson on an egg transporter:

> ...youngsters were in full flow, designing an 'egg transporter' as part of an egg race activity. One came over to the 'materials station' for an egg and asked if the egg was boiled or raw. I paused for a moment and asked 'Why? Does it matter?' 'Oh yes,' came the reply with utter conviction, 'a boiled egg is heavier than a raw egg.' (Watts, 1991, p.47)

The chance remark provided the teacher with information about the students' understanding. It is worth noting, however, that this information would not have been elicited had the teacher answered the question directly instead of posing the question 'Does it make a difference?'. Decisions and actions students make while undertaking tasks like this very often provide teachers with insights into their scientific ideas, which need challenging if they are to develop.

Returning to the parachute lessons, drawing is again seen as a tool for the science classroom. In Chapter 3 there were examples of its being a tool of observation for the study of crayfish. Here it was being used to put ideas into a public arena for others to reflect on them and provided the means of going back to ideas later. It was also used as a means of clarification; having to draw ideas instead of talking about them forces a deeper level of detail.

When students share their solutions with the class as in the case of the testing of the parachute the solutions must be evaluated against the criteria and not judged simply as 'good' or 'bad'. It is here that the art of the teacher is essential in being positive about the uncompleted versions or those that do not meet the specifications. Such difficulties can often arise because a group hit a particularly difficult intermediate problem and time was devoted to its successful solution.

The development of ideas did not stop at the end of the third lesson. Students noted their homework which comprised writing a report of the design brief, design features and giving an evaluation of the effectiveness of their model, including possible reasons for its success or failure.

The fourth lesson acted as a summary and a time to reflect on what had been learned. It was devoted to a discussion of useful design features such as sufficient parachute to reduce the rate of descent, the need for a more efficient parachute as the weight of the egg increased, the need to keep the weight of the container as light as possible while maintaining a structure to take the initial impact (nose cones, tubes landing edge-on) and the suspension of the egg sufficiently high within the structure that after initial impact of the box, the egg has time to slow down sufficiently to prevent cracking. The experience was then linked to design of real problems, such as parachutists dropping from planes, astronauts descending back to earth, or structures on vehicles to take impact. The teacher could of course have introduced the context at the start, talking through with the class how, when a problem is first tackled, ideas are often sorted out by means of a model or simulation; in this case the egg simulating a person.

The evaluation of the product against the criteria is similar to the evaluation of results in the science tasks. But it is also important for the teacher to make students aware that several different solutions were possible and that this is usually a feature of technological problems. The content of the summary session can therefore include judging the end product against criteria, understanding scientific principles behind solutions and becoming aware that there are frequently a number of solutions to a problem. In addition it is possible to consider the involvement of the students in the task and persuade them to articulate what it is like being a technologist or scientist. Students need to realise that the early stages of brainstorming can be muddly and little progress seems to be made; that there are times when what appeared to be a potentially fruitful solution is recognised as unsuitable and has to be abandoned; that persistence in the face of difficulties is often essential; and most important of all, that it is amazing the wealth of ideas that people have if given a chance to think. Discussion like this can encourage students to discipline themselves to face open-ended and often puzzling tasks in the knowledge that their investigation skills and understanding will be enhanced.

Learning how to investigate

The Exploration of Science team at Durham University, researching students' ability to learn how to undertake investigations, analysed the type of knowledge which was necessary for the different stages of an investigation. Their adaptation of the APU model is shown in Figure 4.5, and shows the points of an investigation that draw mainly on students' practical skills, their conceptual understanding and their understanding of procedures. This is valuable for teachers in understanding the demands that these activities can make and in identifying the nature of the problems that students might encounter.

The team produced considerable evidence that where teachers assumed that students would learn procedures by merely undertaking investigations, they met with only limited success. On the other hand, they found that explicit teaching about investigations and procedures was helpful (Foulds, Gott and Feasey, 1992). Their findings support research elsewhere (Gott and Murphy, 1987, Kok-Ann Toh, 1991). Kok-Ann Toh in her account of factors affecting success in science investigations, wrote:

> The substantial difference in the performance of those provided with instruction compared to those without, would attest to the efficacy of the instruction provided. There are two implications for this: first, the teachability of the fundamentals of carrying out scientific investigations, to provide the explicit knowledge necessary to proceed with the investigation; second, that such knowledge would be best served by explicit instruction rather than by mere practice. Undeniably the presence of practice is a vital element after instruction to provide the necessary reinforcement, and it is unthinkable to have instruction without practice for investigative work. But practice alone may not provide sufficient enlightening of some of the fundamental understanding of the nature of scientific evidence.

Researchers have also tried to identify whether the number and type of variables being manipulated contribute significantly to the difficulty of an investigation. They have focused on *independent variables, dependent variables* and *variables which have to be controlled* and additionally described the independent and dependent variables as *categoric, discrete* and *continuous*. In the example of an investigation in Figure 4.3 – How does the rate of blinking depend on activity? – the independent variable is the activity chosen and is a *categoric* variable (it cannot be measured or counted, only described); the dependent variable is the number of blinks which are counted in a given time and is a *discrete* variable (it can only take on whole numbers and is counted). A continuous variable is one which can have a continuous range of values, like temperature, and is likely to be measured with an instrument with a numerical scale.

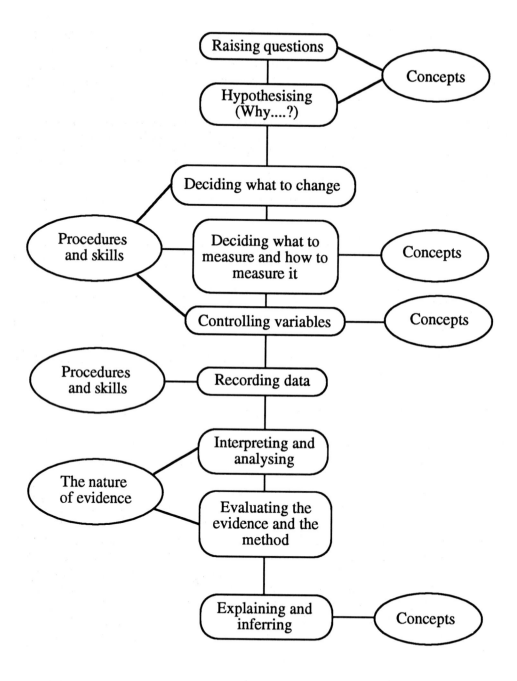

Figure 4.5 Stages of an investigation showing the demands on procedural and conceptual understanding and on practical skills. Origin: Exploration of Science Team to the National Curriculum Council (Foulds, Gott and Feasey, 1991)

Gott and Mashiter (1991) suggest that a move from handling categoric and discrete variables, to continuous variables increases the complexity of a task. Also as the number of continuous independent variables increases so does the complexity of the task. In the examples in the table below investigations in the left hand column show increasing difficulty the further they are down the list.

Investigation	Variables			
	Independent variable	Type	Dependent variable	Type
Which of two jellies dissolves the fastest?	type of jelly	categoric	order of dissolving	discrete
What is the rate of dissolving of two types of jelly?	type of jelly	categoric	time for dissolving	continuous
How does the rate of dissolving depend on temperature?	temperature of water	continuous	time for dissolving	continuous
How does the rate of dissolving depend on temperature and size?	-temperature of the water -size of lumps	continuous continuous	time for dissolving	continuous

Figure 4. 6 Progression in investigations with different types and numbers of variables (Gott and Mashiter, 1991, p. 64)

Learning about the nature of science and technology

In both the scientific investigations and the technological tasks we have included a role for the teacher of helping students understand the nature of the activity, the thought processes which they undertook in tackling the task and their emotional reactions to different phases. There are two reasons for this. The first is psychological and is concerned with individuals' understanding themselves and the way they learn. There is considerable evidence that this sort of understanding leads to more effective learning. The second reason relates to what is being learned. Science education can encompass scientific principles and theories, practical and investigational skills, but it can also encompass a cultural dimension. The latter comprises understanding of the nature of scientific knowledge, its scope and limitations and how it has been built up over time. This was explicitly stated as part of the first edition of *National Curriculum in Science* (1988) in the form of Attainment Target 17 (the nature of science).

> Students should develop their knowledge and understanding of the ways in which scientific ideas change through time and how the nature of these ideas and the uses to which they are put are affected by the social, moral, spiritual and cultural context in which they are developed; in doing so, they should begin to recognise that while science is an

important way of thinking about experience, it is not the only way. (DES, 1988)

Between 1988 and 1992 imaginative attempts were made to help teachers develop this aspect for their work (ASE, 1989). Among these were the importance of students engaging in their own investigations. Although Attainment Target 17 has been removed in the 1992 version of the National Curriculum (a few of the ideas have been woven into the remaining attainment targets), there is hope that this cultural dimension may still remain as a component of science education, through the retention of Attainment Target 1 which requires students to be involved in these small-scale open-ended scientific investigations and technological tasks. This involvement may contribute not only to the development of investigational skills but to an understanding of science as part of our culture.

Foulds, Gott and Feasey (1992) identify the particular cultural element of investigations of helping students understand the nature of evidence:

> Many young people have pre-conceived ideas about scientific issues. The nuclear debate is one example of where pupils allow unfounded argument to influence judgements. Often, their judgements are based on superficial arguments gained from the popular media, or from the opinions of others who are equally uninformed. What it illustrates is that pupils are unaware of the nature of evidence, and of how the evidence, and the reliability and validity of the methods used to collect it, enables us to make informed decisions, whether they be in the context of Sellafield, or in the less demanding context of an investigation to find out which is the best paper towel. In both contexts it is the utilisation of evidence (be it second-hand or otherwise), supported by an understanding of the related scientific concepts, and integrated by the processes which bind the two aspects together, which allows informed decisions to be made.

However, they reported from the research

> The most striking feature of pupils' work is their lack of understanding of the nature of evidence... The overall picture is one in which pupils carry out the investigation well but fail to ultilise the data at all, let alone effectively.

This research influenced the identification of the need for the third strand (see pp.173–5) to Attainment Target 1 of the second version of the National Curriculum (1991). For the purpose of this book, it is important to note the findings of the research and not expect students to learn to intepret data and understand the nature of evidence without help from the teacher. Two examples of how this can be done are described in Chapter 8 on discussions ('Discussion 2', p.165 and 'Extended discussion', p.168).

Summary

The current interest and development in exploring what is possible in this area of the science curriculum is providing a rapidly changing literature on the subject and the potential for further research. Two articles in the December 1993 issue of the *School Science Review* describe recent research in this area and will take the interested reader further. The first by Duveen, Scott and Solomon reports research on children's understanding of the role of theory in science and its link with practical work. The second, by Watson and Fairbrother, summarises findings of the OPENS project, on the management of investigative science in the classroom.

References

Chemical Industry Education Centre (1993) *Making use of science and technology* (Titles: *Fit to drink; Magnox; War against pests; Hydrogen as an energy carrier; Polyfoam; Recycling cities; Wearing jeans; Frozen assets*), CIEC University of York

C.I.E.C. (1993) *Exciting science and engineering for 7–14 year olds*, (18 packs), CIEC University of York

County of Avon Primary Science Working Party (1984) *Working Paper 3: An approach to Problem Solving*, County of Avon Resources (now out of print).

Davis, B. (ed.) (1988) *GASP Graded Assessments in Science Project, Summary Teachers Guide*, London: Hutchinson

Duveen, J., Scott, L., Solomon, J. (1993) 'Pupils' understanding of science: description of experiments or 'A passion to explain?'' *School Science Review*, Dec. 1993, 75 (271), pp.19–27

Foulds, K., Gott, R. and Feasey, R. (1992) *Investigative Work in Science, A Report by the Exploration of Science Team to the National Curriculum Council*, University of Durham

Gott, R. and Mashiter, J. (1991) 'Practical Work in Science – a task based approach?', in Woolnough, B. (ed.), *Practical Work in Science*, Milton Keynes: Open University Press

Gott, R. and Murphy, P. (1978) *Assessing Investigations at Ages 13 and 15*, APU Science Report for Teachers, No. 9

Kok-Ann Toh (1991) 'Factors affecting success in science investigations', in Woolnough (ed.) (see above)

Screen, P. (1986) *Warwick Process Science*, Leatherhead: Ashford Press

Tricker, B.J.K. and Dowdeswell, W.H. (1970) *Projects in Biological Science: Nuffield Advanced Science*, Harmondsworth: Penguin Books

Watson, R. and Fairbrother, B. (1993) 'Open-work in Science (OPENS) Project: managing investigations in the laboratory' *School Science Review*, Dec. 1993, 75, (271), pp.31–8

Watts, M. (1991) *The Science of Problem-Solving: A Practical Guide for Science Teachers*, London: Cassell Educational

Further Reading

Assessment of Performance Unit Science Reports for Teachers
  No 1 Science at Age 11
  No 2 Science Assessment Framework Age 13 & 15
  No 3 Science at Age 13
  No 4 Science Assessment Framework Age 11
  No 5 Science at Age 15

Assessment of Performance Unit Science Reports for Teachers (cont.)
   No 6 Practical Testing at ages 11, 13 and 15
   No 7 Electricity at age 15
   No 8 Planning Science Investigations at Age 11, DES, 1986

Barlex, D., Read, N., Fair, D. and Baker C. (1991) *Designing Starts Here*, London: Hodder & Stoughton

Black, P. and Harrison, G. (1985) *In Place of Confusion, Technology and Science in the School Curriculum,* Nuffield Chelsea Curriculum Trust

Bentley, D. and Watts, M. (1992) *Communicating in School Science: Groups, Tasks and Problem Solving 5–16*, Lewes: Falmer Press

Coles, M. and Gott, R. (1993) 'Teaching Scientific Investigation', *Education in Science*, No. 154, September 1993, ASE

Ditchfield and Stewart (1987) *Technology and Science in the Curriculum: Some Issues and Ideas,* Secondary Science Curriculum Review

Fairbrother, R., (1991) 'Principles of Practical Assessment', in Woolnough (ed.) (see reference list above)

Hewitt, T. and Bateman, R. (1992) *Steps in Technology*, Cheltenham: Stanley Thornes

Jones, A. T., Simon, S. A., Black, P. J., Fairbrother, R.W., Watson, J. R. *Open Work in Science,* Hatfield Association for Science Education

Lee, R. and Aldridge, J. (1989) *Design Briefs: Teacher's Guide and Student's Research Book,* Cambridge: Cambridge University Press

Lock, R. (1990) 'Open-ended problem solving investigations. What do we mean and how can we use them?', *School Science Review*, March 1990, 71 (256), pp. 63–71

Northamptonshire Science Resources (1993) *The Sc1 Book: Investigations 5–16* Northamptonshire Science Centre

Watts, M. and West, A. 'Progress through problems, not recipes for disaster', *School Science Review*, June 1992, 73 (265), pp. 57–63

Wellington, J. (1989) *Skills and processes in Science Education: A Critical Analysis,* London: Routledge

Woolnough, B. (1994) *Effective Science Teaching*, Buckingham: Open Univeristy Press

5
CIRCUSES
Tony Turner

What is a circus?

The term 'circus' was first used in an educational context in the 1960s to describe a type of organisation of lessons in which several different activities (usually, but not necessarily, practical in nature) were set out around a laboratory. For much of the lesson students, often in pairs, tackled each activity, guided by written instructions. It did not matter in which order the tasks were done, nor whether all were completed by every student. The teacher gave an introduction to the lesson and ran a discussion with the whole class at the end. While students were working at the activities the teacher moved from group to group intervening where appropriate. The circus could in some cases extend over two or more lessons. Many examples can be seen in *Nuffield Secondary Science*, published in the 1960s and early 1970s, and in the subsequent *Nuffield 13–16* which was partly derived from it and was published in the 1970s. They continue to be used today.

A circus has to focus on one main idea or phenomenon with all the activities related to the particular focus. One of the best known is the energy circus where students study a wide range of energy transfer devices (steam engines lifting loads, lights driving electric motors via a photocell, falling weights lighting lamps via a dynamo, etc.). A version of this has appeared in many publications after it originally appeared in *Nuffield Physics* (1965). Written instructions are given to explain how to make the gadget work and questions posed that students have to consider.

Exposure to a range of phenomena by itself will not lead learners to an all embracing theoretical idea (see 'The link between practical work and learning scientific theory' in Chapter 3). To perceive the multiplicity of gadgets in the energy circus as examples of energy transfer requires suspension of common sense and an acceptance of abstract ideas. Discussion with and explanation by the teacher are therefore crucial if this is to happen. It was significant that this circus as written in *Nuffield 13–16* had a highly directed framework, with a lot of help as to the appropriate role of the teacher (Schofield, 1976).

A notion of a circus as a set of activities which enables students to arrive relatively unaided at general principles is quite obviously not valid. But if a circus is taken to comprise not only the activities but also the introduction by the teacher, the critical interventions as students work and the discussions with the whole class at the end, it still has an important part to play in the repertoire of ways of organising learning.

Obviously there is the logistical reason for using a circus, in that where there is a need for many short experiences, time, space and equipment constraints make it sensible to provide only one example of each experience and ask students to move round to each one in turn.

More recently and in response to GCSE and National Curriculum, teachers have faced the need to provide problem-solving and investigation activities for students while at the same time 'covering the content' of the syllabus. As shown in Chapter 4 these activities require more time than conventional practical work which can often be fitted into a double period. Thus a tension develops between the need to complete the syllabus and the need to allow time for students to carry out investigations that meet Attainment Target 1 criteria (DES, 1991).

Lock (1991) described responses to this tension in which groups of students tackle common elements of a topic through directed teaching, illustrative practical work, reading of texts, but in which they are also provided with the opportunity to develop one aspect of the topic through open-ended investigations. The range of investigations from which they can choose are devised to appeal to different interests, abilities and pace of working. Lock explains how this arrangement necessitated activities being sequenced over several lessons, with different groups of students working on different activities. Such lessons are, in fact, an extended circus making similar demands on teachers' organisational skills of planning and recording progress. Such an extended circus, in effect, provides differentiation of task by providing different routes through the same material.

Circuses have some features in common with independent learning (see Chapter 6) in that the teacher can move easily from group to group and respond to the different needs of individuals. For success, however, students must see their activities as part of the corporate learning of the whole class, because students often undertake only a few of the activities, for which they must be prepared to take responsibility and report on them to the whole class (see Chapters 4 and 8 for other examples of students reporting to the whole class).

Examples of circuses

A circus requires considerable planning, with clear objectives and calls for a high level of management skills. The decision to use a circus depends on the objectives of the lesson. A range of situations can be imagined for which a circus is suitable and is best illustrated through examples. It may be helpful to readers to imagine the contexts in which the following situations arise and the objectives teachers might have for using them. The examples cover a range of secondary science topics.

Circus 1	An exhibition of materials	Figure 5.1
Circus 2	Kinetic-particle theory	Figure 5.2
Circus 3	Density	Figure 5.3
Circus 4	Extension of senses	Figure 5.4
Circus 5	Isomerism	Figure 5.5
Circus 6	Forces	Figure 5.6

Circus 1 Exhibition of materials

A collection of materials is arranged around the laboratory in the form of an exhibition. It includes examples of natural and man-made materials in the form of raw materials or manufactured articles. The exhibition might include for example: a pressure-cooker gasket, a piece of marble, balsa wood, furnace slag, lump of coal, three-core cable, silicon chip, aluminium nail. Students are invited to examine the objects and speculate on whether they are natural or man-made, whether they are made of a natural or synthetic substance and to suggest some properties of the material. Objects have specific questions by them as shown in the two examples.

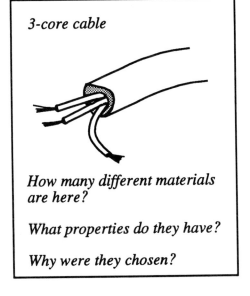

3-core cable

How many different materials are here?

What properties do they have?

Why were they chosen?

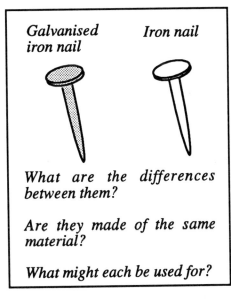

Galvanised iron nail   *Iron nail*

What are the differences between them?

Are they made of the same material?

What might each be used for?

After about 30 minutes the class is reconvened and students report what they have seen and found. The focus of the ensuing discussion includes: classifying materials according to properties, distinguishing between material and object (wood is a natural material, a wooden table is a manufactured object from natural material) and matching materials to use. Questions which might lead to investigations are identified.

Figure 5.1 Circus: Exhibition of materials

The focus of circuses and what can be achieved

The range of situations described shows different ways circuses can be used in science lessons. Within all of them there is considerable scope for the teacher to listen to students, to talk with them and to encourage and direct their activities and conversations. They allow the teacher to intervene and raise the level of discussion. At the same time they provide good opportunities for the teacher to monitor students' progress, to listen and diagnose levels of achievement and quality of thinking and so provide information on which to build later lessons. Hence, the circumstances allow teachers to assess informally knowledge, processes and attitudes.

All circuses must have a clear focus. The first circus, the Exhibition, focuses students' attention on the rich variety of materials and objects. It provides a common experience for all students just starting in secondary school and allows scope for interaction. The different student responses and interactions in small groups enables the teacher to know something of the knowledge the students bring to their science. A circus of such diversity allows students to suggest further investigations, to design other enquiries and hence is essentially open and exploratory in character. Depending on the reaction of students it is possible for the teacher to design a programme of work which capitalises on students' interests, enthusiasms and prior knowledge, linked at the same time to the demands of the curriculum. This circus could be used with a class of very mixed ability.

The second circus on the kinetic-particle theory is very different. Its focus is more specific. Students have to explain natural phenomena in terms of an established scientific theory, to the satisfaction of their peers as well as the teacher. It is explicitly designed to give students practice in using the language of the theory and to explore features of the model. The level of discussion is high in that it deals with the relationship between observation and explanation and requires previous knowledge of both the theory and phenomenon. The circus would probably be preceded by an exposition of the theory. It is likely that the teacher would ask each group to be responsible for one activity, and to give the explanation to the whole class in the second half of the lesson. Many of the phenomena would be ones which the students had met before in earlier parts of their science courses, but it is useful to have the equipment available again as a reminder of what happens.

The third circus provides what has been described in Chapter 3 as illustrative practical work as an introduction to the concept of density. The stations allow students to tackle problems which require, or help to develop, an intuitive understanding of density. The tasks are mostly qualitative or semi-quantitative in nature, and are free from formulae. They are designed to help students become aware that there is an intrinsic property of materials which is independent of size, shape and mass of a particular piece of the material and to help students know the contexts in which the word density is useful. The teacher would be aiming eventually for them to understand implicitly that density is the property of materials not objects.

Circus 2 Kinetic Particle Theory

Each station has a model of the kinetic particle theory alongside a physical phenomenon that can be explained by the theory. The models are all ones that the pupil can handle. Each model has instructions by it, for instance:

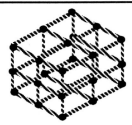

The model crystal at rest represents a solid at zero temperature. As the solid is warmed the particles of the solid begin to move about a mean position. How might this be shown by the model? What happens to the shape of the model? Do the spheres change places? Does the model still represent a solid?

Building a model crystal using polystyrene spheres. In what way is this procedure similar to crystals getting larger?

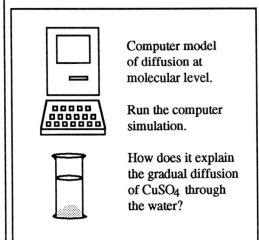

Computer model of diffusion at molecular level.

Run the computer simulation.

How does it explain the gradual diffusion of $CuSO_4$ through the water?

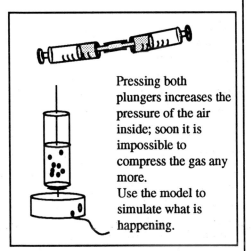

Pressing both plungers increases the pressure of the air inside; soon it is impossible to compress the gas any more.
Use the model to simulate what is happening.

Figure 5.2 Circus on the Kinetic-Particle Theory

Circus 3 Density

This circus requires students to explore a relationship between mass and volume for some systems as a prelude to later work on density. They already differentiate between mass and volume, know the units for both and can use the appropriate measuring instruments.

The stations of the circus include opportunities for students to:

a) compare the mass of equal-sized specimens of different materials by using a simple lever arm balance if they wish. Materials are ranked by heaviness and students are asked to think about the fairness of the comparison. No written report is needed here, although the data are recorded.

b) check the ranking pattern obtained in (a), using a larger, but otherwise similar set of materials. Does the size affect the pattern?

c) look for a pattern between the measurement of mass and volume for a range of regular solids, all of the same material. Students could be asked to devise a way of presenting the readings and to show the pattern in the numbers. Several stations of this sort could be available, using different materials such as wood, plastic and metals.

d) do a bit of detective work. A problem is set asking students to devise a way of showing which one of four solids is made of a different material from the other three. The solids are wrapped in paper, and are of different sizes and mass. A balance and cm ruler is available to students. A report to the class is required showing their decision and the evidence for it.

e) solve the problem 'Which is the heavier, a litre of sea water or a litre of tap water?' Students are given about 100cm^3 of each solution, a balance and a measuring cylinder. Students here are asked to report on the procedure they adopt as well as the result.

Duplicate sets of these five stations should be available, enabling students to do most of the activities in the lesson.

Figure 5.3 Circus: Density

Circus 4 Extension of the Senses

Here a selection of gadgets which in some way may extend our senses is put out. The selection would include magnifying glasses, telescopes, binoculars, hearing trumpets, hearing aids, and a whole range of measuring devices such as feeler gauges, knitting needle gauges, thermometers, etc. Students could be asked to evaluate the devices giving a brief report on how much they extend what can be done with unaided senses. For instance:

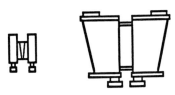

Design a way to compare the performance of the two pairs of binoculars and try it out. Think first of questions you might ask such as :
Are they easy to use?
Are the images clear?
Can you focus them easily?
How much do they magnify?

Find a way of testing the four magnifiers. Think up questions you might ask, such as:

Which ones would be useful for reading small print?
For examining detailed biological specimens?
What can you see which you could not see without them?

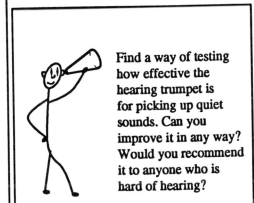

Find a way of testing how effective the hearing trumpet is for picking up quiet sounds. Can you improve it in any way? Would you recommend it to anyone who is hard of hearing?

x20

x100

There are two telescopes available. Telescopes are often advertised as having high magnification; but buyers can be disappointed because the resolution is poor or there is a lot of colour on the image. Compare these two for magnification, resolution and colouring and report on which one you would recommend.

Figure 5.4 Circus: Extension of the senses

Circus 5   Isomerism

Stations are set out with a few molecular models, each showing a different type of isomerism. One part of the display is fixed models which can be handled and reoriented whole; other models at the same station can be dismantled and rebuilt. Information about the substances modelled are given, together with names, formulae and origin. Students have to draw appropriate diagrams to distinguish the isomers, to name compounds and to list criteria for distinguishing between the isomers. After a period the class is brought together for discussion. A key issue in this discussion is the spatial configuration of functional groups of atoms and the concept of symmetry.

Station instructions include:

A) Build a model of the hydrocarbon with a formula C_3H_8. How many different ways can you build it keeping the rules of combination the same? Draw a sketch of your model(s) showing the chain of C atoms in the model.

****

B) Build a model of the hydrocarbon C_4H_{10}. How many different ways can you build it, keeping the rules of combination the same? Draw a sketch of your model showing the chain of C atoms in the model.

****

C) Build a model of the substance represented by the formula C(abcd)) where abc and d represent a different atom or group of atoms attached to the same carbon atom. Use different coloured spheres to represent each group.

Place the model in front of a mirror. Build another model, this time of the mirror image. In what ways are the two models the same or different? Is there a plane of symmetry in the structure?

Finally repeat the exercise for a structure represented by the formula C(abcc); i.e. four groups around the central carbon, two of which are the same.

****

Other stations include models showing other forms of isomerism.

Figure 5.5 Circus on isomerism

Circus 6 Forces

Young secondary students are to be introduced to forces. A useful starter is to let them experience a range of forces in action, noting the effects and feeling the strength of the forces.

Students are given a recording sheet with the station on and asked to go round as many of the activities as possible in the time available and to make brief notes.

a. Feel the force needed to compress the springs and the syringe.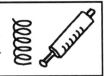

b. What is the force of gravity on the 1 kilogram mass?

c. What force is needed to get this shoe moving across the floor?

d. What is the force needed to pull the door open with the handle?

e. What force can you push with? Try pushing on the scales against the wall.

f. What is the force of gravity on you?

g. Measure the force needed to pull this rubber sucker off the bench using the forcemeter.

h. Compare forces needed to stretch one elastic band and then two elastic bands. Make sure it is a fair comparison.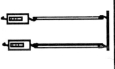

i. Measure the force needed to lift the weight using the single pulley ... and then using the double pulley.

Figure 5.6 Circus on forces

The fourth circus is technological in nature. Students are asked to use the gadgets and evaluate them from the point of view of 'fitness for purpose'. Many of the questions posed ask them to devise a simple 'Which?-type' test to compare one gadget with another. A possible way of running this is to ask the class to try all the devices fairly quickly, to obtain an impression of relative performance and then to call the class together to discuss what is necessary for a more systematic evaluation. This would need measurements to support statements about performance and explanations of how the testing was done. Different groups could then undertake the more systematic evaluation of one of the items or pairs of items.

The fifth circus on isomerism, suitable for an A-level chemistry course, is designed to develop understanding of what isomers are and how they occur. Some people have considerable difficulty in imagining similarities and differences in three-dimensional structures from two-dimensional drawings and hence it is essential that students handle models of the molecules in question. The advantage of this circus is that it draws attention to the range of spatial arrangements possible for molecules with the same formula and allows discussion while students are manipulating models. Students are directed to write and sketch their own notes from the instructions. Teacher intervention is important in promoting discussion and directing thinking. There is less need for a plenary session except of the most general kind. Much of the work will be revisited in later sessions on specific functional group chemistry and the ideas reinforced many times in subsequent sessions.

The sixth circus on forces enables students to recognise a range of physical settings in which it is appropriate to use the word 'force', as well as allowing them to feel the strengths of a range of forces, matching this feel to measurements on a forcemeter. It introduces the unit of force, a newton. Like the circus on density it provides illustrative practical work needed for development of a concept. This last circus has been used in the section below to describe the role of the teacher.

Planning, organising and managing circuses

The production of successful learning experiences calls for a high level of planning and organisation on the part of the teacher and at the same time for the students to work in a particular way, with enthusiasm and commitment on their part.

Planning

A number of considerations arise. What activities might be chosen to meet the aims of the lesson? If one considers say, the sixth circus on forces (see p.107) then the question becomes, what sort of experiences will contribute to the students' understanding of the term force and to their knowledge of what forces do? Selection from a range of activities is narrowed by practical considerations, such as what equipment is available, whether there is a suitable place for it in the laboratory, whether it will be suitable for repeated use by successive groups of students without requiring attention and, of course, whether it is safe.

In setting these activities the teacher has to bear in mind a range of constraints. Not least is the range of performance in the class. The range of activities set must give all members of the class targets they can achieve. Such achievement must include the ability to profit from a whole class discussion about the topic in question; the explanation and summary must have wide applicability. At the same time there should be scope for the more able to progress further and material for the less able to feel a sense of achievement. In addition there is frequently the need to consider bilingual learners who still need support in their use of English. Such support may be given by arranging the grouping to include a bilingual speaker, by the use of support teaching or more often by carefully structured instructional material.

A major factor in setting up a circus is to consider how students will move amongst the activities. Will they be controlled like musical chairs moving from place to place on a signal or will they move as they complete an activity? Embedded within that decision lie other questions. These include:

- Is it necessary for all activities to take the same time?
- Should some activities be compulsory? If so do I need several of those stations so that all students can do them?
- Do I need spare stations for those that finish early and if so, what should they be like? Should they be extension exercises for the more able or provide widening of the range of experiences?

Clearly once a set of decisions has been made, the stations need equipping and setting up. This includes the production of instructions and questions.

Planning must also include deciding what questions might be asked to stimulate students' thinking. These might be: 'Are you pushing on the spring, or is the spring pushing on you?'; 'Why do these instruments, the forcemeter and the bathroom scales, both measure gravity?'; 'Is the pull of gravity the same as weight?'; 'I can't feel anything pulling on me – what makes you think there is a pull of gravity?'; 'What is holding the rubber sucker down so hard? It isn't very heavy and the water we put on to help it stick is not usually used as a glue.'; 'If I hung a weight on two forcemeters together what would they read?' There is usually no point in writing questions like these on instruction sheets; it is best for the teacher to judge at the time the best moments to use them.

Introduction

The introduction must involve and interest the class in the topic in hand, have clear statements of purpose and adequate instructions about what has to be done. It must not be too long to allow time for the circus activities and the discussion at the end. If the circus on forces were being used as an introduction to the topic of forces, it would be necessary to elicit from students the sort of understanding they already had, by posing questions or instructions such as:

'Where have you used the word force?'
'Write ten sentences using the word force.'

These might be listed and discussed, in order to distinguish the contexts in which force is used in a physical sense from those in which it is used in a psychological sense.

The purpose of the practical activities would then need to be made clear. From the teacher's point of view the aims might be that the students:

- experience forces, getting the feel for different sized forces;
- use new measuring instruments;
- become familiar with a new unit – the newton;
- record information briefly;
- have opportunities to make predictions and test them.

Students might be asked to record on their sheets what the activities had in common and what was happening in the system when forces were applied. The use of a simple record, which encourages students to write what they find interesting or any measurements they make, is all that is needed at this stage to help the plenary session.

Finally students need to know:

- where to start,
- when to move on to the next station,
- what to do if there is no room at the compulsory stations,
- any safety precautions,
- how much time they have.

During the activity

During the practical session the teacher will be looking for information about the level of understanding of the topic, the sorts of questions the students are asking and generating information that will allow him or her to conduct a useful plenary session. The teacher will be moving from group to group in order to promote discussion, keep the conversations along acceptable lines and field questions. This becomes a time for the teacher to use some of the challenging questions thought about at the planning stage.

At the same time there will be the need to keep an eye on all that is happening, to monitor overall movement around the stations and deal with those pieces of equipment that appear not to be working properly. It might also be possible to monitor process skills but with the range of practical activities in this circus there may be more than enough to keep the teacher occupied.

Finally, of course, there is the need to decide when to stop. It is a matter of judgement how many of the activities need to be completed. As long as some key ones are included by all, the discussion session can make sure all students are aware of what is going on. Stopping and clearing is important, so that adequate time is left for a discussion of the events. It is a common mistake of beginning teachers to let practical work go on for too long for the sake of getting everything done. One result of that decision is to leave the discussion for the next lesson. This may occur several days later by which time the events have lost their impact and immediacy and students may have forgotten both content and purpose.

Bringing ideas together

After the practical activities students can be brought around the front bench to share their observations and ideas. A selection of the activities can be collected on the front bench to be used as the focus of the discussion and for further demonstration if necessary. It is often useful to get a group to report, inviting comment by the others. As well as developing confidence in the students and nurturing the ability to present ideas, it provides for the teacher further insight into the students' understanding. The opportunity arises to encourage and praise and to add to or modify the report for the benefit of all. Doing this without putting down students or devaluing their contribution is a skill not all teachers have. A record kept on the board allows this development of ideas and findings to be shared by all. For those who are reluctant or poor at reporting care is needed to boost confidence by encouragement and choosing the appropriate activity for them to report.

But it is important to recognise that this topic is one where the teacher has to take the students beyond immediate sensory experience into abstract ideas. This cannot be done merely by the students reporting. The challenging questions used during the circus with individuals will be important here. Demonstrations, not only of the items which formed part of the circus, but of related phenomena would be useful. For instance, many students find it difficult to understand how pulleys work; but there is a simple demonstration using a rope tied on one piece of dowel rod and passed over another, and then back again which could be used here.

Students should go away with a clear picture of what has been learned and an appropriate record. In this example of the forces circus much of what has been learned is experiential, with a fairly limited written record of the practical activities. As the focus of the lesson was on understanding forces, an appropriate exercise to follow would be marking both direction and position of forces on drawings of situations in which forces are acting.

In dealing with responses to a range of circus activities the teacher will have to be prepared to deal with a range of reactions from the students when it comes to discussing what they have seen or understood. Despite structuring a work station it is common experience that several students, as with a group of adults, can each take very different views of the same phenomenon. The teacher has to value each student's response, to focus on the positive aspects of a report and to direct it towards the aim of the lesson. This requires considerable skill, fitting each student's contribution into the aim of the lesson.

Photographic record of a circus used in a lesson on interference

The circus illustrated by plates 5.1–5.8 was on interference in light and water waves. The activities involved observation of interference phenomena in light (soap films and soap bubbles); interference in water waves (ripple tank);

Circus: lesson on interference of waves

Plate 5.1 Demonstration of interference of waves to the whole class

Plate 5.2 Using students to help with the demonstration

Circus: lesson on interference (cont.)

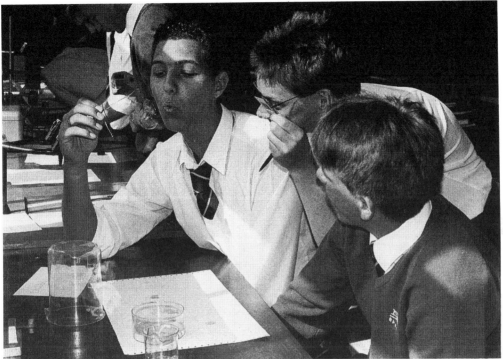

Plate 5.3 Making soap films and viewing them through filters

Plate 5.4 Teacher clarifying instructions

Circus: lesson on interference (cont.)

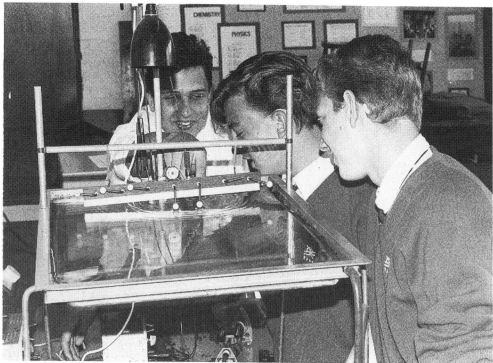

Plate 5.5 Studying interference in water waves in a ripple tank

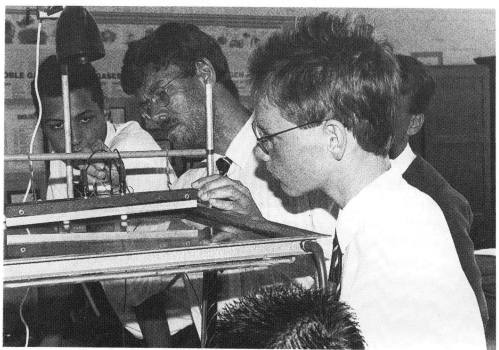

Plate 5.6 Teacher adjusting the equipment

Circus: lesson on interference (cont.)

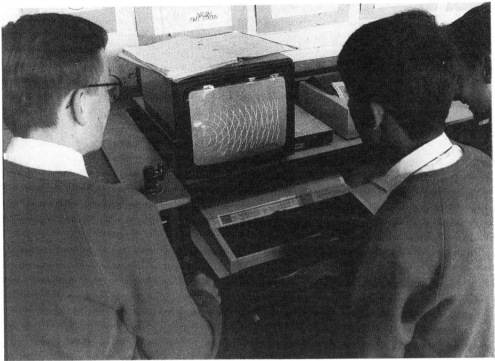

Plate 5.7 Using a computer simulation of interference

Plate 5.8 Computer print-out of interference of waves

computer model of interference where the programme allowed alteration of both wavelength and distance of separation of sources. Some of the teacher's time was taken in adjusting equipment to give the best effect (plate 5.6) and in clarifying instructions (plate 5.4). Before the circus the teacher had given an explanation of interference using the model plastic waves (plates 5.1, 5.2). This has some similarities with the circus on kinetic particle theory where students are trying to relate explanation to phenomena. The use of the circus goes hand in hand with exposition and demonstration to the whole class.

Summary

The teaching functions that circuses fulfil vary considerably and it is worth here referring back to the chapter on practical work. Circus 1 on materials provides mainly an observational practical, where questions are used to draw students' attention to particular features and where questions raised by the students are noted and used for study later. The focus of Circus 2 is on theory rather than practical, because it is requiring students to engage in the task of linking the explanation of particle behaviour at 'microscopic' level to the macroscopic behaviour of gases and liquids. Circus 3 is an illustrative practical experience where the activities and questions have been selected to help the teacher develop a particular concept. Circus 4 requires students to use skills associated with investigations, because they have to decide how to evaluate the gadgets which have been supplied. Circus 5 is a theory lesson, where students have to manipulate concrete models of theoretical models. Circus 6 provides students with a range of practical experiences, which will be used as the springboard to abstract ideas. The questions the teacher asks and the discussions that ensue are key to forming the link between observation and theory. The circus on interference shown in the photographs is basically an observation-type of practical activity, where students are seeing what interference effects look like in practice. It is, however, significant that the teacher explained interference first, so that students knew and understood what they were looking for (see Chapter 3, the link between observation and theory).

Like any activity which allows students to control their own learning, to work at their own pace and to make sense of phenomena for themselves, a circus can be highly motivating with potential for developing personal responsibility for learning. On the other hand there is the danger that students drift and fail to understand the significance of each task. A teacher must therefore strike a balance between allowing students to work on their own using their own initiative and providing enough structure to give direction. Hence activities within a circus are chosen by the teacher and the circus as a whole has a specific focus.

References

DES (1991) *National Curriculum in Science*, London: HMSO

Howard, E. (1971) *Nuffield Secondary Science Theme 4*, *Harnessing Energy*, York: Longman

Lock, R. (1991) 'Open-ended, problem-solving investigations – getting started' in *School Science Review*, 72, 261, pp. 67–73

Schofield, B. (1976) *Nuffield 13–16, Energy, Teacher's Guide and Pupils' Guide*, York: Longman

6
INDEPENDENT LEARNING
Leslie Beckett

Introduction

Schools can be pretty unnatural environments for children's learning. We assume too readily that children's interest and involvement can be switched rapidly from a project on local history to a study of photosynthesis at the sound of a school bell, that thirty varied individuals can cope with the same diet of science at the same pace, and reach roughly the same end point after an eighty-minute dose of teaching. In this chapter we shall explore ways in which, within the inevitable constraints of school organisation, the learning process can be made more flexible, and can take account of the individuality of children and their different styles of learning. Also, exploring ways of making children more responsible for their own learning will force us to ask basic questions about the role of the teacher.

Definitions

Many terms are used to describe the methods and styles of more individual approaches to teaching and learning and it may help to suggest some definitions.

Individual learning describes a student working alone as opposed to working in a group. The learning can be purely receptive learning or it can be discovery learning, it can be closely prescribed or open to student choice. It can occur when students are all working at a common task but as individuals within the class. It will occur even in the most inflexible situations when children respond to a 'pain in the head' because in the end for all of us learning is about that personal assimilation of the world and trying to come to terms with new ideas and experience.

Individualised learning is a term to describe a situation where learning objectives and activities are tailored to individual needs, capabilities and interests and often involves different pace and styles of working.

Independent learning emphasizes that some responsibility for organising and decision-making has been transferred from teacher to student. It can operate on a short-term scale for specific tasks or it can be a long-term and total approach to learning. Responsibility and accountability are implied whenever students are given an opportunity to work independently.

Resource-based learning emphasises the **direct** access to sources of information, guidance and stimulus in contrast to receiving them through the mediation of the teacher.

Supported self-study is a term increasingly in use. It places learning in the domain of individualised and independent study but emphasises the context of support that is necessary, not only through the provision of resources but also through tutorial support at a personal level, in helping students to organise their work, thought, experiences and values.

The connotation of independence and individualisation might suggest that such learning cannot thrive within the confines of a class-based, timetable-based organisation and requires a total alternative to traditional schooling. Such an alternative is possible, but our task is to examine how this approach and emphasis can be grafted on to existing systems to increase the teacher's repertoire and give students a wider experience of ways of working and learning.

The Educational Justification

The detailed educational arguments on independent learning can be found elsewhere (Green, 1976), but let us here briefly summarise reasons given by practising teachers for their involvement in C.E.T. Supported Self Study project (Waterhouse, 1983).

The thinking which underlies their commitment contains a number of separate but related components:

i   belief that it is the responsibility of secondary education to educate the whole person, to treat children as individuals and to help them to become autonomous;

ii   a conviction that individualisation will result in more effective learning;

iii   a desire to create in classrooms an atmosphere that is supportive rather than confrontational and domineering;

iv   a belief that schools have an important task to help students to learn how to learn.

The teachers' wish for autonomy for their students (reason i) is an acknowledgement that accepting responsibility for their own learning is a vital training towards maturity and an important recognition by adults of their worth as individuals.

The conviction about the merits of individualisation (reason ii) is a recognition of the reality of individual differences. Cognitive differences themselves are multi-dimensional and complex; in addition, children mature intellectually at different rates, the knowledge they bring to the learning task varies, they have different interests and aptitudes, different styles of learning, and their performance in school is powerfully influenced by the home and community background. For some, practical work and concrete examples of phenomena are the crucial experiences in learning. Some depend strongly on assimilating written material which for others presents a formidable barrier. We have not recognised adequately the initial effect of the different rates at which students assimilate ideas. Many students spend their school lives almost getting to the point of understanding when the clouds of uncertainty disperse, and then they are rushed on to a new topic, ending up with only a hazy understanding of a lot of ideas. How much better it would be if we gave them the chance to grasp half as many ideas really well.

The use of an independent learning approach does not exclude group experiences and teacher-led elements, but the teachers responding with reason iii are obviously aiming for a 'working with' model to ensure less distant and impersonal relations in their lessons.

The concept of 'learning to learn' is not new, but it has received renewed attention with the increasing importance of 'information skills' in an era of new technology, and with the realisation of the limiting effect on chidren's learning of the absence of training in study skills. The National Foundation for Educational Research (NFER) study on 16–19 study problems (Dean, 1978) was followed by the growth of special study skills courses at this level; but the real solution must lie in embedding the development of those skills within the learning material itself. The Inner London Education Authority (ILEA) independent learning courses in A-level Sciences have successfully incorporated this training within their course material. The ABAL project (A level Biology), for example, chose to make study skills training particularly prominent as an aim in the first unit of the course (ILEA, ABAL, 1980). The importance of 'learning to learn' was stated by HMI:

> If, as seems likely, changes in employment and technology are as rapid as forecast, retraining and re-education may well become part of everyone's expectations and entitlement. Schools can lay an invaluable foundation by equipping young people with the skills of independent study. The ability to handle programmes of work which are dependent on a variety of written, audio-visual and programmed media sometimes provided at a distance from an educational institution as well as a range of tutorial contexts may become an essential prerequisite for the future. (HMI, 1985)

Finally, to these four concepts of autonomy, individualisation, personal relationships and 'learning to learn' must be added another argument for more flexible learning, namely the efficient use of the teacher. Whatever way lessons are structured and resources used the teacher will remain the key resource for learning. The question to be asked then is:

> 'How can other resources be provided so that the teacher is freed to do those things which only a teacher can do?'

If a structured programme of argument and questioning can guide a student to an understanding of an important idea in science, for example, the relationship between molecular speeds and the pressure of a gas (ILEA, APPIL, 1990), then a teacher need not spend time at the blackboard writing out a formal explanation

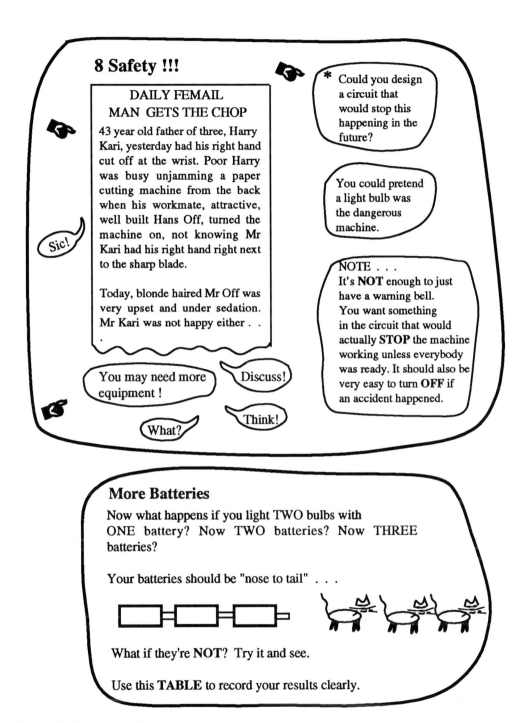

Figure. 6.1 Examples of task cards

with varying success to the whole group but instead can be free to deal with individual difficulties and motivation.

Releasing a teacher from the role of simply transmitting information provides the time for the more important roles which will be discussed later.

Elements of Independent Learning Material

1. Objectives
It should be very evident that teaching by whatever method requires that the teacher has thought out clear anticipated outcomes of knowledge, understanding and skills and found ways of sharing these appropriately with the students. Education (root meaning 'leading') ought not to be a game in which students are expected to tag along without knowing why or where they are going. Everything is to be gained by letting children into the teacher's confidence, and these signposts become indispensable if students are given independent learning material.

2. Study Guide
A guide towards these objectives. At the minimum this may be no more than a suggested route through a range of standard resources, or conversely it may be a course book with a detailed exposition of the topic as, for example, the ILEA A-level Chemistry (ILPAC, 1983–4). The guidance may be through *structured exercises* which often incorporate a series of questions (with hints and answers); for example, a series of slides of cloud chamber photographs can be viewed and the questions will guide the student through the process of discovering the significance of this information in the way that the original scientist had to proceed.

Some independent learning material supplements this heavily structured guidance with more loosely structured guidance through a set of *Task cards* (Figure 6.1). Basic experimental work on electrical circuits could be structured by a series of Task cards which provide for alternative routes; often one task, while providing explanations, leaves the student with an unresolved question which can be addressed by selecting the next task to meet that need.

Hint cards are another way of providing guidance but only when students recognise the need for it. In a problem solving activity which involves designing a parachute, hint cards might be available such as:

Hint

What difference does it make if the parachute
has a hole in the top? Try changing the size
of the hole.

Figure 6.2 Example of a hint card

3. Feedback

A key to motivation and guidance in independent study is provided by regular questions which serve to reassure and check on learning. The big adjustment that students have to make in feeling at home with independent learning is that of recognising that they can learn without the constant leading of a teacher. This only comes through the reinforcing feedback of success, even partial success in answering regular check questions. So building in feedback is vital; it is often achieved through regular punctuation with self-assessment questions, and access to answers which may be full explanations, hints or even further leading questions. Students can then learn quickly to 'play the game', to treat the questions not as examination items but as a self-check; to use the answers wisely after a serious struggle with the questions as a means of confirmation or correction.

4. Resources

Later examples will set the use of resources in context. Here we need only stress that resources must be appropriate and varied. Students should have access to alternative explanations of ideas (a range of books on the laboratory shelves), and find variety in their learning through interacting with experimental work, models, audio-visual material and computer software.

Plate 6.1 Independent study area with a library which provides access to a range of resources including film, video and microcomputers

Plate 6.2 Use of independent resources during a lesson

5. Final Assessment Checks

Independent learning needs to be organised into manageable chunks of work, which for older students may be several weeks long, but particularly for younger students will be much shorter, only a lesson or two. At the end, before taking a deep breath and starting something new, there is a need to check how far objectives have been achieved. So time should be found to put away the crutches of open books and someone else's answers, and for students to answer questions which test the achievement of objectives – questions set to check mastery. These answers will be for teacher-marking and will form the core of regular guidance by the teacher through tutorial support.

Ways of Using Independent Learning

The argument for individualisation in learning does not depend on an all-or-nothing solution. Successful schemes operate with comprehensive use of independent learning in science and mathematics at all levels in secondary schools, and examples will be referred to later. But there are ways in which modules of independent study can be incorporated within a varied and flexible approach to teaching, ways which acknowledge that strongly directed, teacher-centred class teaching is inappropriate, particularly as a follow-up to primary school experience, where children have had more responsibility and freedom in their learning.

Teachers using independent learning recognise the need to give students time to adjust to it to avoid a sense of isolation and uncertainty. Perhaps all students adjusting to this way of working have to go through an uncertain phase, but there comes a point where they realise they are making progress even though the teacher is not 'up front'. Such reassurance only comes as they achieve success in their assessed responses, and part of the teacher's role is to encourage them through uncertainty to the point where they enjoy the freedom of working in this way. Perhaps short but regular experience of independent learning is the best way to build up students' confidence in their ability to be independent, but teachers should not regard temporary uncertainty as a sign of the permanent failure of this approach.

Implicit to the successful working of independent learning is a well organised set of resources. For a scheme of work based around a sequence of workcards the students will need a map of the scheme with its alternative routes and a set of workcards carefully and clearly filed in a laboratory cabinet.

Other programmes may be based on a unit booklet which suggests possible references and resources. For this a tray of books, pamphlets, games, etc., could be collected and made available over a series of lessons to the students working on that unit. Trays also provide a means of storing the collected equipment and materials for particular experiments. If this proves problematic because of the need to have equipment available for a range of classes then the aim should be to identify the resources which are very specific to one bit of independent learning material and ensure that this is labelled with reference to the particular unit of work while locations of general equipment are well displayed in the laboratory. The test for any successful organisation of resources is how effectively students are able in the rush at the end of a lesson to return these things to their correct location ready for their next user. Perhaps a 'signing off' register would encourage some commitment to this handing-in process. Of course, the teacher cannot change her role to tutor/course planner for each individual merely by placing a large collection of resources at the disposal of students.

A system of management must be developed in the laboratory which enables her to:

    (a)   create time to consult (teach) individual students,
    (b)   keep track of and monitor the wide variety of activities in the laboratory,
    (c)   assess some students' work and
    (d)   gauge the right time to introduce whole group activity.

A system of management must be judged by how well it enables the teacher to become the major effective learning resource.

A system which has grown out of the work of the Avon Resources for Learning Development Unit and been tested by many teachers involves students in 'study tours'. Each tour begins and ends with a consultation, however brief, between teacher and student. The major components of such a system are:

1. Consultation	to review and plan ahead.
2. A record card	to record work done, assessment and observations on the work, a profile of achievements and future plans.
3. A task card bank	which guides students to activities and resources.
4. A master plan	giving a synopsis of task cards and a flow chart of suggested routes through.
5. A resource bank	books, videos, slides, pamphlets, and equipment for practical work.

The relationships among all these elements can be illustrated by Figure 6.3.

Other decisions which teachers have to make, implicit to some independence, are about the organisation of students working at very different rates. The system outlined above envisages a situation where individual students are going at their own pace, within a well-planned system of recording individual progress and regular teacher intervention at a personal level for each child. However, there are other possibilities. The whole class can be set a fixed period for a module of work, and within that time a 'core and extension' pattern of activity will help to provide for the range of abilities and rates of working. Dividing the class into small groups of four to eight children is another possible compromise to facilitate management; often such groups form spontaneously. If groups are designated it should not be assumed that they are inevitably to be homogeneous. It is possible for very successful groups to operate in which there is diversity, in

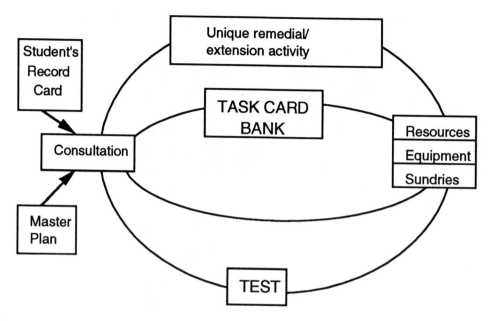

Figure 6.3 Key elements of resource-based learning

which peer group teaching can develop; groups within which very different targets are achieved by individual students around a common learning task.

So a possible pattern of development which would incorporate individual study might be like that of Figure 6.4.

Stage 1	Introductory lesson (or part)	Introducing the topic and ways of working Fixing the common task
Stage 2	Group tutorials	Groups planning a task and the teacher involved in turn with small groups
Stage 3	Independent study phase	Teacher support now at individual level
Stage 4	Debriefing and rebriefing	Group tutorials for students to discuss achievements and plan new assignments

Fig. 6.4 Stages in the learning cycle

Plates 6.3–6.8 were taken of an A-level group working with the independent learning course ABAL. Although the members of the group were at different stages there was one occasion where they came together to undertake a joint practical exploration on breathing (plate 6.4).

A-level Biology class using ABAL, an independent self-study guide

Plate 6.3 Teacher providing feedback

Plate 6.4 Independent learning is more than just studying books:
variety of learning experience is crucial

A-level Biology class using ABAL, an independent self-study guide (cont.)

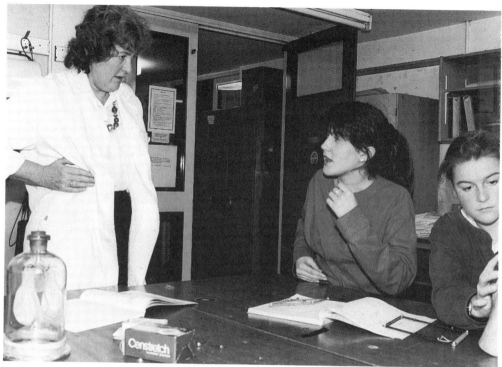

Plate 6.5 Teacher discussing breathing mechanisms with one girl

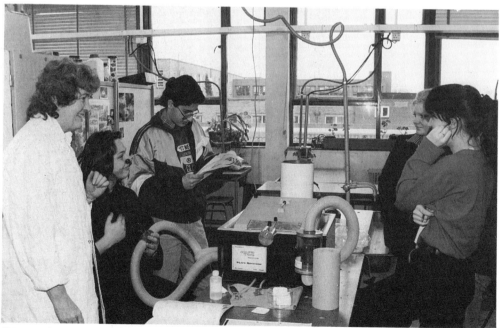

Plate 6.6 Peer group teaching and the teacher's guidance

A-level Biology class using ABAL, an independent self-study guide (cont.)

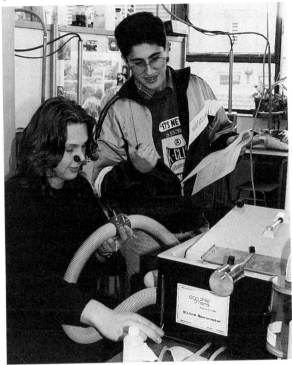

Plate 6.7 Collaboration in learning is part of independent learning

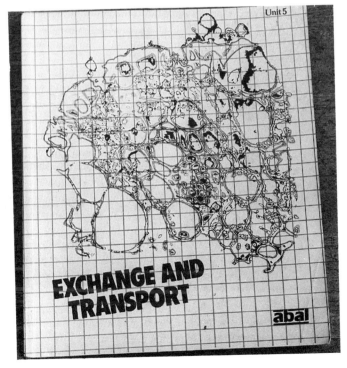

Plate 6.8 ABAL Study Guide

A-level Biology class using ABAL, an independent self-study guide (cont.)

Plate 6.9 Teacher monitoring progress in the whole class

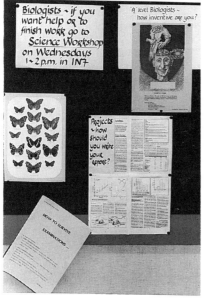

Plates 6.10, 6.11 Displays also support independent study

Some Examples of Independent Learning

While it is important to look for generalisations about management patterns for all kinds of independent learning and search for helpful guidelines which have a wide applicability, it will be useful now, in contrast, to describe some specific examples of independent learning material found across a broad age range of students.

A. Seeds on the move

A Y8 module, presented as a small A5 booklet and produced by a girls' comprehensive school in South London, has the following four sections:

1. Plants and their problems

   a) Directed reading: a word search of key words and their meaning
   b) Group discussion on the problem of seed dispersion: write down the problem
   c) Group discussion on possible solutions: write about it
   d) Practical activity with selection of fruits and seeds, including classification
   e) Follow-up of homework sheet on classification and extension sheet.

2. Moving through air and water

   a) Reading of resources (four books named and others available) on wind dispersion and air resistance
   b) Individual answering of questions and discussion of answers in small groups
   c) Experiment on parachute
   d) Homework: making an annotated chart of seeds and their dispersion methods.

3. Animals dispersing seeds

   Activities leading to a wall display, possible cartoon strip of a conversation between plants on methods of dispersion (see Figure 6.5) with a chance at the end to summarise all the related ideas by making a spider map of the topic.

4. A project on fruits and seeds (see Figure 6.6)

   a) Preparatory work for the project through tape/slide
   b) Collection of fruits and seeds and research on information about these
   c) Investigations – series of questions/problems, some of which can be solved by 'fair tests', some by questionnaire to family and friends, some by search of written material
   d) Assessment. Clear explanation given of how the project will be assessed and an invitation to students to write their own honest report on the project.

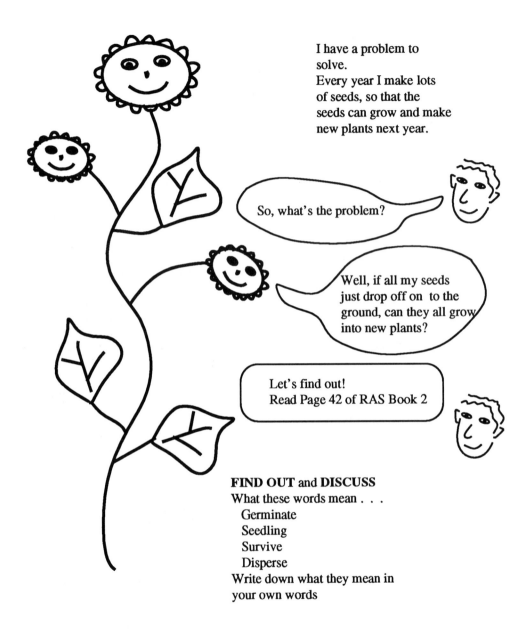

Figure 6.5 Plants and their problems: independent learning material

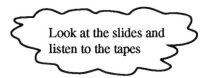

A PROJECT ON FRUITS AND SEEDS

Collect as many **DIFFERENT** fruits and seeds as you can. It's a good idea to collect a leaf at the same time.

FIND OUT the names of each one (there are plenty of books to look in...)

DECIDE how each fruit and seed is dispersed.

MOUNT your collection in an **INTERESTING** way. By each fruit or seed, you MUST write its name,
   describe HOW it is dispersed, and
   explain WHY it is dispersed like that.

e.g.   **SYCAMORE** - the seeds are dispersed by the wind because they have two wings which catch any breeze.
* **OTHER THINGS**   you could include in your project

You could do some **INVESTIGATIONS** of your own to find out the answers to these questions. Some of them you could find out for homework.

1. How far do sycamore seeds travel on a windy day?

2. Which seeds travel the furthest through the air?

3. How many different fruits do we eat? Where are the seeds in the fruits? Are they always easy to spot?

4. How many exotic fruits can you find in the market? How would their seeds be dispersed?

5. Do all seeds float equally well?

6. What DID happen at Krakatoa?

7. Which seeds do animals like best?

NOTE - If you do an experiment, you will need to **PLAN** it carefully making sure it's a **FAIR TEST**. What do you want to find out? How will you do it? How are you going to set out your results?

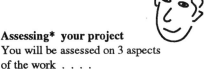

Assessing* your project
You will be assessed on 3 aspects of the work . . . .

Presentation
a) The general impression -
    Is the work neat?
    Is it well laid out?
    Does it look interesting? *(6 marks)*

b) Have you used your imagination?
    How original are your ideas? *(5 marks)*

c) How much work have you done?
    The minimum amount?
    Or have you put a lot of effort to produce good work? *(6 marks)*

Figure 6.6 Project on flowers: independent learning material

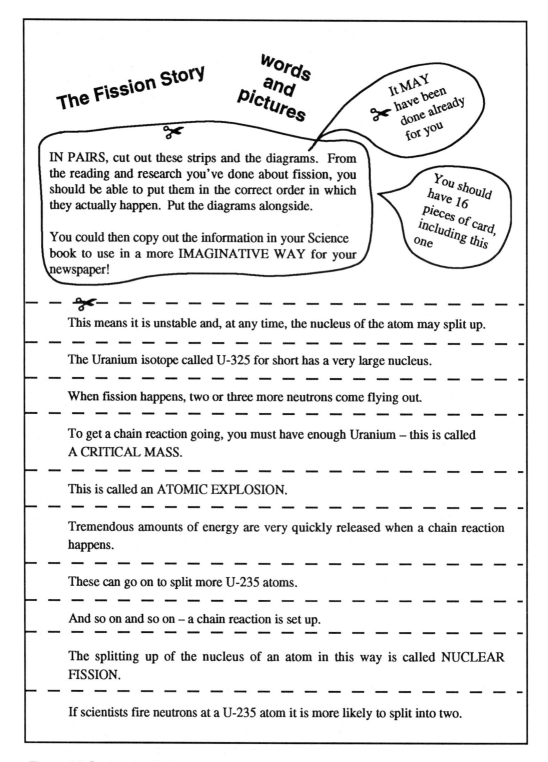

The Fission Story

words and pictures

It MAY have been done already for you

IN PAIRS, cut out these strips and the diagrams. From the reading and research you've done about fission, you should be able to put them in the correct order in which they actually happen. Put the diagrams alongside.

You could then copy out the information in your Science book to use in a more IMAGINATIVE WAY for your newspaper!

You should have 16 pieces of card, including this one

This means it is unstable and, at any time, the nucleus of the atom may split up.

The Uranium isotope called U-325 for short has a very large nucleus.

When fission happens, two or three more neutrons come flying out.

To get a chain reaction going, you must have enough Uranium – this is called A CRITICAL MASS.

This is called an ATOMIC EXPLOSION.

Tremendous amounts of energy are very quickly released when a chain reaction happens.

These can go on to split more U-235 atoms.

And so on and so on – a chain reaction is set up.

The splitting up of the nucleus of an atom in this way is called NUCLEAR FISSION.

If scientists fire neutrons at a U-235 atom it is more likely to split into two.

Figure 6.7 Sorting the fission story

In this short piece of structured learning there are many opportunities for individual work, a sharing of problems and solutions among peers, encouragement to learn through books, tapes, slides and experiments, individual imaginative writing and the challenge of planning careful investigations. The motivation is maintained by planning all this to culminate in a small but significant project as a means of consolidating previous understanding and providing scope for individual and group activities.

B. Nuclear Issues – a cross-curricular project

An independent learning programme for Y11 girls produced at the same London school has a very different format. This project in Science links with studies in History of the Second World War and leads to the production of a newspaper by each group of girls; so the design department have become involved in developing ideas of lay-out and illustration. The girls show a lot of motivation in tackling the task because they say it is about the real world, and it gives them an opportunity to work at their own pace and make a lot of decisions. The end product allows for a great variety of contributions from features like 'The Child's Guide to the Atom' to articles on 'A Nuclear Winter'.

The introduction to the work is through a set of thirteen A4 cards beginning with a set of objective questions 'What do you know already?' – a pretest in nice disguise. Opportunities are provided for group discussion of the introductory fact sheets leading to the formulation by individuals and small groups of a set of questions to which they want answers during the study. These are kept as one of the guides for further work so that this time it is not the teacher's questions that set the agenda but those of the students. The structure is deliberately loose to encourage diverse tasks, but all the students will be prompted to do plenty of reading (there are over 20 information sheets and many references to a collection of books). There are suggested activities to follow up the reading, questions to answer and answers to discuss in groups. In addition there are videos to view on topics like Nuclear Power Generation, Radiation Hazards. The suggested activities along the way develop from not-too-demanding tasks like ordering a set of statements on Nuclear Fission (see Figure 6.7) to more demanding arguments on social aspects of science; and all is clearly leading to the building-up of knowledge and confidence to be effective reporters in the final task. Topics covered in this study include Atomic Structure, Radioactivity, Nuclear Fission, Effect of Nuclear Fall-out, and time is allowed to express personal anxieties created by some of the issues as a group task and in a teacher-led tutorial.

C. APPIL – A-level Physics Project Independent Learning

By contrast to the previous examples this is a published course in eight units with a teacher's guide and student handbook covering the full requirements of a two-year course. APPIL does not claim to be a text book, but rather a structured guide to a range of resources. This is made apparent by the inclusion (along with the familiar self-assessment questions) of Study questions which can only

Q 1.2 Study question

(a) In a typical metal, what is true of the outer-most electron(s) of each atom? Explain why it makes sense to think of these as being 'shared' between all the ions in a piece of metal. How can the movement of these electrons be described? Why are they often referred to as 'free electrons'?

(b) When a potential difference is produced between the ends of the conductors an electric field is set up in it. Describe what effect this has on the free electrons, and explain why they do not get faster and faster. Why are the free electrons also called 'conduction electrons'?

(c) What happens to the energy transferred by the electric field to kinetic energy of these electrons? What observable change corresponds to this?

(d) What is meant by the 'drift velocity' of the conduction electrons? If we think of these electrons as being similar to the molecules of a gas, what does the drift velocity correspond to?

Using references in answering a study question
References are given at the beginning of each chapter. Some are to general physics text books, others are in books concerned mainly with electricity. In all the references given you will find parts which are relevant to a particular question. There are two ways of dealing with this efficiently.

1 Using the *index*. To do this, you will need to read through the question, decide what you want from the reference, and note the *key words*. Question 1.2, for example, is about the movement of electrons, and you will find index references to 'conduction electrons' or 'free electrons' in several books.

2 Use the *sub-headings* to find relevant sections of the chapters. Read through these sections and make brief notes of the points you want to include in your answer.

For more help on how to make notes, consult the APPIL Student's Handbook and read the relevant chapter in *Use your head* by Tony Buzan.

Figure 6.8 Study question, APPIL

be answered effectively by using the reference texts. The early study questions in the course (see Figure 6.8) are also used as a vehicle for developing study skills (one student admitted: 'Until I studied APPIL I had never used an index...'). Development questions are also used to free the teacher from having to explain standard arguments, and the answers to this kind of question guide students towards confidence in making the argument their own. Individual study is enhanced by group work during the course through performing experiments and discussing together responses to comprehension exercises. Questions based on objectives are provided at the end of each chapter, allowing important check-points for tutorial intervention.

The Place of Personal Interactions

It will be clear from the quoted examples that in schools episodes of individual learning occur in the context of a social group, and the development of these interactions and relationships with peers and teachers are essential elements of intellectual and emotional growth. Students working on independent tasks will nevertheless discuss common difficulties; they will consult and be involved in peer group teaching (all the more if the teacher is not dominating the lesson) and there will be opportunities to plan and perform experiments together. This group interaction in between periods of individual work has clearly been strengthened in the examples given by planning group discussions, common tasks and peer group assessment.

Plate 6.12 Independent learning, but learning together through a common task

The other crucial interaction in this method of learning is that between teacher and student in a 'tutorial'; the word has to be used to describe a wide range of situations. In a lively class of first formers the encounter may be brief and highly structured with one eye on the rest of the class throughout. But there has to be a recognition of the need to find time in each lesson to see some of the students on an individual basis to monitor progress and record new goals. With smaller groups of older students the tutorial will be more leisurely and more individually tailored. Often part of the agenda for such a tutorial will be suggested by the course itself, but an effective tutorial will generally contain some or all of the following elements:

1. Re-establishing and strengthening relationships
2. Review and evaluation
     • student reviews and evaluates completed work;
     • teacher responds to this evaluation, and invites comments on this from
        the student;
3. Forward planning
     • teacher stimulates interest in new work; helps students to create
        'advanced organisers' of subject matter;
     • works with student to create a plan of work;
     • fixes deadlines for completion (guidance adapted to abilities, interests
        and working style of student);
4. Confirmation
     • teacher summarises tutorial contract, and gives the student opportunity to
        add his own summary of the transaction.

The Teacher's Role in Independent Learning

As teachers, at least for part of the time, move from the front of the class and become managers of independent learning they need to adapt to new ways of working, possibly even more than their students. Perhaps the best training for a teacher is to adopt the role of a student for a day, take an Open University unit and discover how she can learn this way, where her motivation originates, how she reacts to feedback elements and when she feels in need of support. It is the art of appropriate intervention above all that has to be learned. When a student is absorbed in a task the last thing he may welcome is a teacher enquiring about progress; at another time what may be most needed, without being realised, is a crucial suggestion from the teacher to unblock a mental jam. The examples of independent learning described earlier indicate how removing teachers from the role of information dispensers leaves life as hectic as ever as they timetable themselves into new jobs.

The initial task is that of **organiser** of the learning material. Much of this organising precedes the students' study. Even when a module has not been developed by the teacher there is need for thorough familiarisation with the material, learning where difficulties can be anticipated, identifying points where teacher input would be appropriate. Much of the richness of good independent learning depends on the quality and variety of the resources; this assumes much work will be done by teachers in selecting reference books and apparatus, finding magazine articles, identifying suitable videos and computer software. They must then become sufficiently familiar with this selection to be able to exploit its potential.

The teacher has to be the **guide** as students embark on unfamiliar territory. Examples have been quoted of the way individual study can be set in a context created by the teacher in an introductory briefing session to the whole class. Students working through a structured programme can easily become so involved in just coping with the next hurdle that they see only the trees and not the wood. Teachers can guide the learner beyond the detail to the larger pattern of ideas. This can be achieved by setting the scene with the whole class at the start of a module as well as at the end of a section, when students can be made aware of the more significant ideas and how they relate to other ideas in the course. The teacher is also a guide to individual students, pointing them towards a particularly helpful reference or suggesting an alternative way of tackling a problem.

Only the teacher can help to **motivate** and encourage when students are struggling or failing. This role is particularly vital in the early stages of readjustment to new ways.

Plate 6.13 Making time for individuals – vital personal contact for monitoring progress and encouraging motivation

The teacher is also required to **monitor** students' progress. This demands a management plan enabling regular assessment of the student's work, such evidence then being drawn on as the basis of tutorial support.

Earlier, a possible tutorial format was outlined to include discussion of assignments and fixing of future deadlines within the context of an agreed contract with the student. Deadlines are important. We all work to them, and students need them to plan their commitment to foreseeable goals. The flexibility of independent learning allows deadlines to be fixed appropriately for each student on the basis of clear knowledge of the student. The monitoring and assessment role of the tutor can be combined with the other roles of guide and organiser within a management cycle such as suggested in Figure 6.9 (see also CET Self-study Project (Waterhouse, 1983)).

The tutor briefs the student, helping to plan the next phase of work, and mutually agreeing a contract with objectives clear and deadlines explicit. Then follows a period of individual learning when the student uses resources and obtains the support and encouragement of the teacher. The learning is reviewed at the next stage of the cycle and this assessment provides feedback to students and reviews their progress before moving on to a stage of further briefing and a new contract. So the cycle is completed, and shows how tutorial intervention relates to the whole cycle of management.

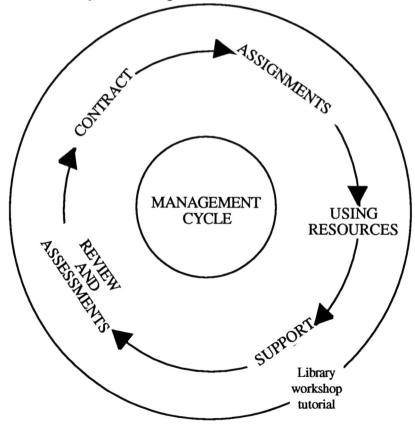

Figure 6.9 A management cycle for independent learning

This management cycle will be an individual artefact for each student but the teacher will use her judgement in deciding which elements in the cycle can be dealt with in a group context. Independent learning can never be implemented by launching students into unknown territory and leaving them to sink or swim. The key aims should be to encourage student autonomy while at the same time freeing the time of the teacher to remain the crucial resource. So there will be important times within the independence when the teacher can set the context for learning and can inject special enthusiasms and insights to enhance motivation.

References

Dean, J. (1978) *16 – 19 Study Problems*, Windsor: NFER

Green, E. (1976) *Towards Independent Learning in Science*, London: Hart Davis

Haines, C. (1989) 'Experiences with ILPAC: individual learning in supported self study' *School Science Review*, 70 (253), p.107, ASE

HMI (1985) *Report on Resource Based Learning*, London: HMSO

ILEA ABAL (1980), *A level Biology Alternative Learning*, Cambridge: Cambridge University Press

ILEA APPIL (1990 Revised) *Thermal Properties*, Chapter 3, London: John Murray

ILEA ILPAC (1983–4) Independent Learning Project in Advanced Chemistry, London: John Murray

Waterhouse, P. (1983) *Supported Self Study in Secondary Education*, Council for Educational Technology

7
SIMULATIONS
Sheila Turner

Ladies and Gentlemen I should like to welcome you to this Public Meeting of Radleigh Town Council. The Council has to decide whether fluoride should be added to our water supply. Before we make our decision we should like to ask you, the public, to let us know what you think... I shall be calling upon Dr Sanderson, our Medical Officer, to tell us the view of the experts...

The start to the meeting of the Radleigh Council to consider whether or not fluoride should be added to the local water supply was calm and civilised. The Medical and Dental Officers proceeded to outline the reasons why fluoride should be added; the scientific evidence pointed to the many benefits to dental health which could accrue, including a reduction in dental caries in the population. The debate which followed was at times heated. The scientific evidence was enough to convince the local trades unions of the merits of the scheme; the local residents were concerned about the cost; the Group against Compulsory Medication considered the plan an infringement of individual liberty and Sid Jones, a local pensioner, remained unconvinced by all the arguments, he knew fluoride was a poison.... The meeting ended in uproar. Would the Council decide to proceed with the plan in spite of the strong opposition?

The meeting described above could be one which might have taken place in any part of the country. In reality it was a simulated meeting which took place in a school as part of a programme developed to help students understand more about social and technological applications of science; it could also have been used as part of a health education programme or in English or social studies lessons.

What Are Simulations?

Before considering the part simulations can play in science lessons it may be helpful to consider what is meant by the term simulation. In the broadest sense simulations can be thought of as activities which 'mimic' real situations. The activities can take many different forms some of which, like role-play, have long traditions in drama in many regions of the world. Simulations which are used in teaching can be divided into a number of types including:

role-play, where participants take on the roles of individuals in specified situations, such as the Council meeting which introduces this chapter. The roles can be improvised or students can use a script; role-play focuses attention on the interaction of people with one another.

simulation games include simulations which may involve elements of competition, and also include board games which are based on real-life situations.

computer simulations, which permit modelling of real life situations on a 'micro' scale and which utilise the facility of computer programs to reproduce experiments/processes which cannot be undertaken in the school laboratory because of time, expense or safety considerations.

Simulations, particularly role-play activities, have been used in a variety of ways in education for a long time. Dance and drama often call upon younger students to 'pretend to be...'. Such activities have a valuable role in helping children to develop their understanding of science concepts as well as helping them to come to terms with emotions, such as anger, which are of importance in developing personal relationships. Eleven-year-olds working as groups to simulate the working of gears, or the way in which sound travels through the ear, can be helped to understand scientific concepts as well as developing social skills, including those needed to work together in a shared enterprise. Such activities may help students, particularly those whose first language is not English or those with learning difficulties, to communicate their observations, and to understand scientific phenomena in far greater detail than would be possible in spoken or written form. For some students such activities may provide a way 'into' science: sometimes this occurs through the increase in confidence and self-esteem which role-play activities afford. The activity may also help students to recognise the 'human face' of science. Very importantly such activities can lead to significant gains in knowledge and understanding for all students.

Simulations provide a mechanism for modelling reality in the classroom setting, free from the constraints of the real world, and are therefore a teaching strategy which has wider application than just in the teaching of dance and drama. Simulations can enable young people to explore complex issues in a secure environment where it does not matter if mistakes are made. This is particularly true of computer simulations which enable students to distance themselves from the real situation. Simulations are also infinitely adaptable: they can operate at any level and with students of any age or ability. In their most sophisticated form they include small enterprise initiatives; for example, those developed as part of the Technical and Vocational Educational Initiative (TVEI), as well as the complex War Games used by Government Departments to develop defence strategies.

The advent of the wide use of microcomputers in schools in the past decade has created opportunities to use simulations in new contexts in science. The increasing sophistication of computer graphics has led to a new generation of simulations, such as 'Slick' (1983), which employ moving, coloured images and screen layouts which incorporate text and pictures that can be varied according to the needs of the user. Computers and computer simulations are also a familiar element in the lives of many students. The amusement arcades full of sophisticated machines which permit young people to drive racing cars round Brands Hatch or new-style museum exhibitions, such as those in the

Natural History Museum in London which allow exploration of, for example, human physiology and inheritance, are but two instances of the possible experiences which students may have had of computer simulations. This familiarity with simulations can be used to advantage when students are being encouraged to think about the limitations of simulation programs and the models on which they are based. Simulations have more recently been extended to include those programmes which allow users to create their own models (Rogers, 1990; Ogborn, 1990), and it would be appropriate to include also the use of spreadsheets for modelling (Brosnan, 1990).

The development of the 'Domesday' Project has stimulated the production of interactive simulation programs linked to video material. The *Ecodisc* (BBC, 1986), for example, enables users to explore the dynamics of a natural environment and to examine ways in which changes, both planned and unplanned can affect a particular habitat. The program also permits evaluation of the likely outcomes of decisions made by students. This type of program may herald a new era of simulation programs for use in schools.

Selecting Simulations for Use in Teaching

Decisions about whether or not to use simulations during a particular class depend on a number of factors; most important of these will be the learning outcomes which it is hoped to achieve and the appropriateness of any material to be used.

> – Does it fit in with the topic being taught?
> – What learning will occur as a result of using the simulation?

Most published simulations include information about learning objectives, including those related to knowledge and understanding, which enable learning outcomes to be identified easily.

For those who have never used simulations before it is usually advisable to select published material, particularly those already tried and tested by colleagues. It takes time to develop successful simulation activities – time is of the essence! Also, using materials that have been developed and tested enables those who have not tried simulations before to avoid some of the pitfalls. Where published materials do not quite meet the needs of a particular group it is generally possible to modify them fairly easily. Colleagues, including those from other departments such as Drama, English, History or Geography, will probably be able to provide other examples of activities which they have used which could be modified for use in science – a variant on the Limestone Enquiry role-play exercise in the Association for Science Education's *Science and Technology in Society* materials (ASE, 1988) has been used by geographers for many years. Such interdepartmental discussion also ensures that any overlap in teaching a particular topic is planned rather than accidental.

An important consideration in planning, including the selection of appropriate activities, will be the prior experience that students may have had of simulations, as well as their age and ability. In role-play activities in particular, the emotional maturity of both individuals and the group as a whole has to be considered when choosing simulations. The experience that students may have had in Drama or English can often be utilised as well as the expertise of colleagues in these departments. Y10 and Y11 students may explore ideas concerning self-image and esteem in Drama, which could be linked, for example, to discussion of anorexia nervosa in Science. Role-play activities which involve students coming to terms with emotions require sensitive handling; joint ventures with other colleagues who have had experience of using role-play can be helpful. A difficulty which sometimes arises is that students who have engaged in role-play in drama may not relate this experience readily to the science laboratory. Students who have never engaged in role-play activities in science before may feel threatened by the different and unexpected demands suddenly being made of them 'out of context'. However, some students respond to the challenge of taking on new roles in new contexts in a very positive manner. Such experiences can enable students to revise the negative images of science which may have hindered their learning. These activities can also be a way of making science more accessible to children with specific learning difficulties, particularly those who have difficulty in expressing ideas through the written word.

Other factors which have to be considered include the time needed for running the simulation and the availability of suitable rooms. Most simulations, apart from short role-play activities, require at least an hour to run. The use of computer simulations may require booking of equipment and it may be necessary to organise room changes. Laboratories with fixed benches do not always allow flexible use of space although is is amazing how much can be achieved with a limited floor area. Even traditional laboratories permit activities which involve students moving around to illustrate what happens, for example when blood from an incompatible blood group is introduced into the body. Constraints such as the ones outlined above mean, however, that it is rare to be able to use simulation on the spur of the moment.

The following check-list, and the summary of the processes involved in planning a role-play, which are summarised in Figure 7.1, may be helpful in selecting materials:

- Does the material fit into the topic being taught?
- At what stage in teaching the topic can the simulation be used most effectively: as an introduction? as a reinforcement or extension? as a revision?
- Is the material appropriate for the age and ability of the class?
- What experience have the class had of using simulations?
- Will the materials have to be modified in any way?
- Have other colleagues used this material before?
  How did they use it?
  What did they think of it?
- How long will the exercise take?
- How much duplicating is needed?
- What additional materials or equipment may be needed?
- Can the activity take place in the normal laboratory/room?

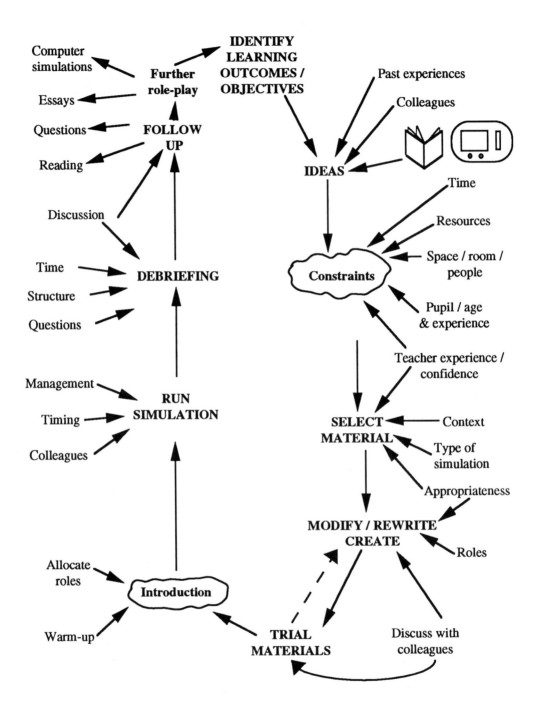

Figure. 7.1 Using role-play in Science

Using Simulations in Science

As has already been indicated, the successful use of any simulation depends, as does so much in science teaching, on careful planning of material before the lesson and effective classroom management during the lesson. This section looks in turn at the types of planning, classroom management and debriefing needed for using role-play, simulation games and computer simulations in science lessons.

A. ROLE-PLAY: 'Fluoridation'

1. Planning and organisation of role-plays

What happened before the Radleigh Council met to decide whether flouride should be added to the water supply? Some of the important elements involved in the planning of the 'Fluoridation' role-play are shown in Figure 7.1. The planning and organisation before the lesson can be subdivided into four elements:

> i) Choosing and preparing materials
> ii) The environment
> iii) Time
> iv) Allocation of roles

i) Choosing and preparing material

The material for the role-play was chosen to help students to identify:

> a. the reasons for adding fluoride to the water supply, particularly those related to dental health based upon scientific evidence and data,
> b. the ways in which scientific knowledge and data can be questioned,
> c. the complexity of the decision-making process.

One of the major outcomes is related to knowledge of dental health, particularly the causes and prevention of dental caries in children and adults. In this role-play it is helpful for students to have some prior knowledge of the subject material; it provides a useful extension or reinforcement exercise in years 10, 11 and 12.

The role-play was developed from 'Fluoridation of the Water Supplies,' one of the *Science and Technology in Society (SATIS)* units (ASE, 1988) and 'Finding out about Fluoride' (Schools Council/ Health Education Council Project, 1982). Although these materials are designed for a discussion they can readily be developed into a simulated meeting at which the points for and against fluoridation are argued. A public meeting enables all students in the class to be involved in the role-play – an important consideration! There is the possibility of any number of people, including students absent during the preparation of the lesson, to act as members of the local council who ultimately make the decision about whether or not fluoride will be added to the local water supply. Some key roles, such as Medical and Dental Officers who put forward the 'scientific' case for fluoridation, allow for 'assistants' so that small groups can work on the development of the case for a particular organisation or group. Such group work allows for discussion and learning to occur during the initial stages before the actual role-play takes place; it also permits sharing of roles – an important consideration for those who lack confidence. The sharing of roles also reduces the number of role descriptions which have to be written out and duplicated. The role descriptions can be colour-coded to help in the general organisation and running of the role-play and to ease filing of materials for future use; putting the descriptions in plastic wallets also makes them more durable.

ii) The environment

A public meeting like 'Fluoridation' can easily take place in a laboratory. The chairperson and the major speakers need to face their audience, so they can be accommodated behind a demonstration bench or table at the front of a laboratory. The remainder of the class can sit at benches in the same way as they normally do. Although some role-play activities necessitate the rearranging of furniture, students are very skilful at coping with apparent limitations imposed by laboratory design which includes fixed benches and little space for movement.

iii) Time

Simulations of public meetings usually call upon a large number of people to speak and therefore require at least an hour to run. Time is also needed for introducing the activity and for preparation. The preparation can be limited to a single lesson to allow students to read the background information, discuss it in small groups, and make decisions about who will make particular points during the actual meeting. The possibility of a homework period for additional preparation can be helpful. The preparation may also include a lesson which raises issues, for example, the possible effect of the addition of flouride on wildlife – would excess fluoride be removed at the sewage works? Time also has to be allowed for discussion after the role-play ends – the all-important debriefing, which may take as long as the role-play itself.

iv) Allocation of roles

The way in which this will be done depends on the class and the nature of the role-play activity. It is particularly important to ensure that the whole class participates in the activity; a public meeting like the one called by Radleigh Council is ideal as additional roles can be created easily. In some instances students may allocate roles themselves, but this is not always appropriate. Whatever method is adopted the system chosen needs to be perceived by students as 'fair'. Pieces of paper with names of the characters written on them can be used, volunteers called for or parts allocated by teachers. Sensitivity is needed in allocating roles; younger students tend to become closely identified with the part they are playing and some may not find it easy to cope with the

Lesson: Role-play: Public meeting on fluoridation of water

Plate 7.1 Role-play – even in a laboratory with fixed benches

Plate 7.2 Distributing roles – answering questions

Lesson: Role-play: Public meeting on fluoridation of water (cont.)

Plate 7.3 Going round helping

Plate 7.4 Preparing roles

Lesson: Role-play: Public meeting on fluoridation of water (cont.)

Plate 7.5 The debate 'We think it's wrong to make people drink water with fluoride in it...'

Plate 7.6 Debriefing – the final vote

emotional demands of certain situations. Although such experiences can be a valuable part of a student's development they can also cause distress, particularly in role-play situations allied to health education which may relate to personal relationships or experience. Our knowledge of individuals gained from observing them in a variety of situations, allied to discussion with other staff, is invaluable when making decisions about who should play a particular role – the quietest member of the group in science lessons may reveal unexpected talents when asked to chair a meeting.

2. Classroom management of role-play

Management for role-play activities can be likened to that of a stage manager in a theatrical production. The 'play' has been written, the parts assigned to the players, the production is in the hands of the players or their chosen producer. The stage manager's role is to stand back and not to interfere – and that often calls for restraint! In this situation the teacher is the facilitator, an adviser who provides information and support when needed, who boosts morale through praise and encouragement – this last is particularly important for all students but especially for those who are uncertain and diffident. The good stage manager is alert at all times to signs of distress or occasions when players cannot handle the emotions aroused; at such times it may be necessary to intervene, perhaps in an assumed role, to diffuse a situation. In 'Fluoridation' the teacher became a member of the Council and was able to intervene, where necessary, by asking questions. In this situation the notebook and pencil, essential for noting points to bring out during the debriefing which followed, were part of the Council member's role and thus less obtrusive.

3. Debriefing role-play – What have we learnt?

The final stage of any simulation, and one of the most important elements, is the debriefing in which the outcomes are discussed, analysed and evaluated by the participants. It may also include students coming to terms with emotions, such as anger, aroused during the exercise. Ideally the debriefing should occur at the end of the lesson; if this is not feasible it should occur as soon as possible after the role-play. Sometimes a brief period of discussion at the end of the lesson can be followed by written comments by students allied to time in subsequent lessons devoted to more analytical discussions of the issues raised. However the debriefing is organised, it normally takes at least as long as the time spent running the simulation; it may take much longer.

What follows an activity of this type will depend on whether the simulation was used to introduce a topic, as a central feature, as summing up or as revision. The follow-up may include a range of activities (see Figure 7.1) including further role-play or refining the original material.

Finally, teachers should not be disheartened if the first time they use a role play they think the lesson was a disaster! Different groups respond in different ways to new experiences – the same activity will probably be successful with the next group. It is worth persevering, talking to colleagues in the Drama and

English departments and asking them for help. Running role-play activities does become easier with experience.

B. SIMULATION GAMES: The Nitrogen Cycle Game

Games are an intrinsic element in the lives of most children, they are an important factor in learning life skills and one from which many derive considerable enjoyment. It may seem strange, therefore, that their role in schools has been confined to sports lessons, clubs and end of term 'treats'. One reason for games being an under-used resource almost certainly lies in the element of competition which forms a major ingredient of most games. Other factors, such as the dearth of good, readily available material and the time needed for such activities, have also prevented teachers exploring the potential of simulation games as a learning activity, particularly in science. Their potential for motivating students, encouraging and reinforcing learning, has too rarely been explored; nor has their possible role in assessment been considered – the school which used a simple 'Energy' game (ILEA, 1989) as a means of self-assessment is unusual. Harnessing students' creative talents in developing their own games is even more uncommon – which seems unfortunate as such activities can provide a mechanism for creating and sustaining interest as well as giving opportunities for children to clarify their thinking about scientific concepts.

1. Planning and Organisation of Simulation Games

i) Choosing and preparing material

Undoubtedly the most important questions have to be considered in choosing a game for use in science are:

> Is this the best way of teaching this topic?
> Will the game facilitate learning?

The answer in the case of topics like the nitrogen cycle is that a game which draws together different elements of the cycle and the effect of human activities on the environment – such as the use of nitrates as fertilisers or in industrial processes – may well be the most suitable way of helping students from 13 to 16 years to learn about complex inter-relationships.

Games like the Nitrogen Cycle have other features to commend them. It is one of a number of simple games which are included in published science textbooks (Lythe and Gray, 1986) or teaching materials (SATIS, 1988 and ILEA, 1989); it is therefore readily available at a reasonable price. It can be used without the need to prepare and duplicate material. The instructions for the game are on the same page as the board, the only requirements for each group of four students are a die, counters (it is suggested that coins could be used) and beads, for example, for nitrogen 'tokens'. Although there is an element of

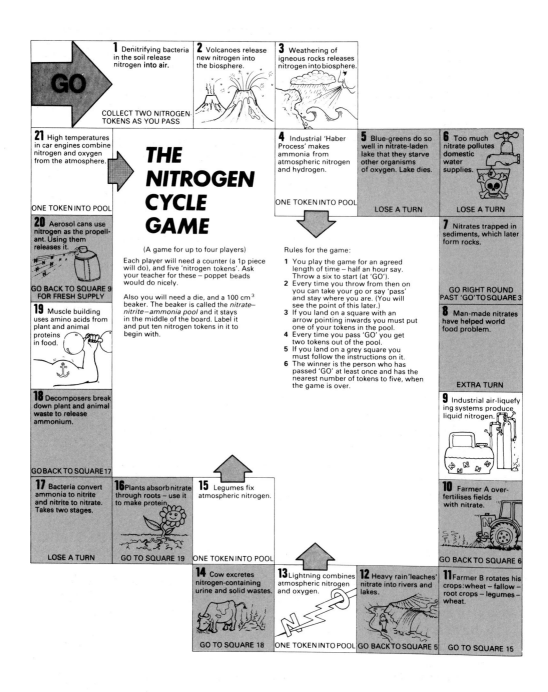

THE NITROGEN CYCLE GAME

(A game for up to four players)

Each player will need a counter (a 1p piece will do), and five 'nitrogen tokens'. Ask your teacher for these — poppet beads would do nicely.

Also you will need a die, and a 100 cm³ beaker. The beaker is called the *nitrate–nitrite–ammonia pool* and it stays in the middle of the board. Label it and put ten nitrogen tokens in it to begin with.

Rules for the game:

1 You play the game for an agreed length of time — half an hour say. Throw a six to start (at 'GO').
2 Every time you throw from then on you can take your go or say 'pass' and stay where you are. (You will see the point of this later.)
3 If you land on a square with an arrow pointing inwards you must put one of your tokens in the pool.
4 Every time you pass 'GO' you get two tokens out of the pool.
5 If you land on a grey square you must follow the instructions on it.
6 The winner is the person who has passed 'GO' at least once and has the nearest number of tokens to five, when the game is over.

GO — COLLECT TWO NITROGEN TOKENS AS YOU PASS

1 Denitrifying bacteria in the soil release nitrogen into air.

2 Volcanoes release new nitrogen into the biosphere.

3 Weathering of igneous rocks releases nitrogen into biosphere.

4 Industrial 'Haber Process' makes ammonia from atmospheric nitrogen and hydrogen. ONE TOKEN INTO POOL

5 Blue-greens do so well in nitrate-laden lake that they starve other organisms of oxygen. Lake dies. LOSE A TURN

6 Too much nitrate pollutes domestic water supplies. LOSE A TURN

7 Nitrates trapped in sediments, which later form rocks. GO RIGHT ROUND PAST 'GO' TO SQUARE 3

8 Man-made nitrates have helped world food problem. EXTRA TURN

9 Industrial air-liquefying systems produce liquid nitrogen.

10 Farmer A over-fertilises fields with nitrate. GO BACK TO SQUARE 6

11 Farmer B rotates his crops: wheat – fallow – root crops – legumes – wheat. GO TO SQUARE 15

12 Heavy rain 'leaches' nitrate into rivers and lakes. GO BACK TO SQUARE 5

13 Lightning combines atmospheric nitrogen and oxygen. ONE TOKEN INTO POOL

14 Cow excretes nitrogen-containing urine and solid wastes. GO TO SQUARE 18

15 Legumes fix atmospheric nitrogen. ONE TOKEN INTO POOL

16 Plants absorb nitrate through roots – use it to make protein. GO TO SQUARE 19

17 Bacteria convert ammonia to nitrite and nitrite to nitrate. Takes two stages. LOSE A TURN

18 Decomposers break down plant and animal waste to release ammonium.

19 Muscle building uses amino acids from plant and animal proteins in food. GO BACK TO SQUARE 17

20 Aerosol cans use nitrogen as the propellant. Using them releases it. GO BACK TO SQUARE 9 FOR FRESH SUPPLY

21 High temperatures in car engines combine nitrogen and oxygen from the atmosphere. ONE TOKEN INTO POOL

Figure. 7.2 Nitrogen Board Game

competition the goal is to maintain an equilibrium in the system by making skilful decisions. The instructions suggest that the game should be played for a predetermined length of time, which means that timing for a lesson is relatively easy. As the game forms part of a textbook, it is easier to use it as part of a normal lesson sequence; follow-up activities are also suggested which enable students to use what they have learnt to draw diagrams which illustrate the nitrogen cycle.

The basic principle of games like 'The Nitrogen Cycle' could be adapted for other situations; even this game may need to be modified for developing bilingual or less able students as, although the board has pictures, the text may be too complex for some students. Rules for the game need to be kept as simple as possible. In producing or adapting materials, it is worth trying to make them attractive and durable, for example by colouring and/or mounting material on coloured card and laminating with transparent book-covering material.

ii) The environment

Games like 'The Nitrogen Cycle' where students are working in small groups can take place in most laboratories with little or no rearrangement of seating. The only requirement is space for the board (in this case an A4-sized sheet of paper) and room for students to sit around it.

iii) Time

Lack of time is often a reason given for not using games as part of lessons. It is true that some games, for example the 'Pond Dipping Game' (Cade, 1986), which simulates relationships in a pond and can be played at different levels of complexity, requires at least forty-five minutes. 'The Nitrogen Cycle', however, can be played for a predetermined length of time and this allows the game to be used more readily as part of a normal lesson. Time in this case is not a constraint and therefore debriefing discussion can take place at the end of the game.

2. Classroom Management of Simulation Games

Classroom management for games is far less complex than for role-play activities. 'The Nitrogen Cycle' can be used by small groups with all students involved in the exercise at the same time or as part of a circus of activities. Once groups have been organised and the game started students generally become totally absorbed. The rules for this game are relatively simple – which means that arguments about cheating are minimised. Most board games are suitable for small groups of students – generally four or six at most – so where materials are limited the game may have to be used as part of a circus of activities, which may include other games.

3. Debriefing of Simulation Games

The form and length of the debriefing will vary according to the type of game used. 'The Nitrogen Cycle' is normally played for thirty minutes, which means that discussion about what students have learnt can usually take place in the same lesson. The game itself provides a focus for the discussion, for example, about the affect of human activity on the environment and the alternative strategies which can be adopted in, for example, farming practice. Suggestions for extension activities are also provided – drawing a diagram of the nitrogen cycle using the material presented in the game. Follow-up work could also include asking students to develop their own game based on another topic which they have already studied, for example, the water cycle.

C. COMPUTER SIMULATIONS: 'PEG' and 'Moving Molecules'

'Quick – move PEG upstairs – that window in the bedroom is open...all the heat's escaping...now put the radiator on...' Computer simulations, like 'PEG', can produce a high level of involvement and interest and have a place in science education.

The choice and management of computer simulations is similar in some respects to that of other types of simulation. However there are some major differences. Role-play activities focus on the interaction between individuals and groups whereas a computer simulation involves interaction between an individual, or small group, and the computer program. The emotional involvement which occurs is thus very different; the individual is distanced from the situation being simulated and this means that management of the learning experience is easier as outcomes are more predictable.

'PEG' (British Gas, 1983) and 'Moving Molecules' (Cambridge Educational Software, 1983) provide examples of two different types of computer simulations. 'PEG' is designed for students from 10 to 13 years to understand the factors which affect heating in the home; it involves decision-making skills and incorporates an element of competition – successfully keeping the house at a suitable temperature permits students to score points. 'Moving Molecules' allows secondary students to investigate the behaviour of molecules in gases, liquids and solids.

1. Planning and Organisation of Computer Simulations

i) Choosing the right material

Both 'PEG' and 'Moving Molecules' provide examples of programs which can be used in a variety of contexts: 'PEG' could be used as an introduction or as an extension for work on energy; 'Moving Molecules' is useful both in introducing and in revising concepts linked to the kinetic-particle theory. 'Moving Molecules' consists of a number of discrete sections which permit users to model the behaviour of molecules under different conditions, for example, temperature and pressure; it could therefore be used for teaching different age groups. Programs of this type which allow flexibility of use, which model situations which cannot be demonstrated under normal laboratory conditions, and which permit prediction of outcomes, have much to commend them.

The question of what makes a good program is not always easy to answer – particularly when sophisticated graphics and use of colour, such as those in 'PEG', ensures that students will enjoy using a program whatever its value as a learning aid. Questions such as:

What will children learn from using this program?
Is this the best way to teach this topic?
What are the limitations and sophisitications of the mathematical model upon which the program is based?

are helpful in assessing whether or not to use a particular program. In some programs a 'random factor' is incorporated so that the program more nearly approximates to the real situation – this may be an essential element in programs which model biological systems. Some programs have a facility which enables parts of the program to be modified so that they can be used more flexibly and this can be of use in modifying them to meet the needs of particular groups of students.

Trying out the program personally before using it with a class is obviously a 'must', but it is also sensible to evaluate any accompanying material, including instructions and exercises or worksheets. Some programs, like 'PEG' and 'Moving Molecules', are 'free-standing' and do not require additional materials to be duplicated; the information needed to use the program is presented on the screen.

Colleagues who have used the program will be able to provide help on its value in helping students to understand particular concepts and on how to use it more effectively. Reviews of programs which appear in journals, such as the *School Science Review* (ASE), are also valuable in helping to identify appropriate material. Unfortunately, it is generally impossible to acquire programs to review prior to purchase in the same way as books.

ii) The environment

In an ideal world computers would be available in the laboratory to be used when needed as an adjunct to a lesson or be readily available in the room next door. The reality varies from school to school but rarely approaches the ideal. In many schools computers are housed in particular rooms which have to be 'booked' for class use. The use of computers thus becomes a special event rather than an integral part of normal lessons. It also means that students may be working in a room with which they – and perhaps you – are less familiar and this can cause difficulties unless you have planned for all eventualities!

Bringing computers into the normal teaching area also needs to be planned carefully – is there space for computer(s) to be positioned in such a way that small groups can sit to use the controls and see the monitor readily? If it is possible to have only one computer in the laboratory/classroom 'Moving Molecules' could be used either as part of a circus of activities, as described in

Chapter 5, or as a class demonstration where the computer is linked to a larger monitor so that the whole class can see the screen.

iii) Time

One of the perceived problems with using computers is the amount of time required, particularly to run programs. Time is needed certainly for preparation prior to the lesson, to run through a simulation program and to test it for the 'bugs' which will be found when the 'creative' student is let loose! Such preparation time is normally less than thirty minutes. If students are using a program for the first time they need time to familiarise themselves with how the program works, to 'play', and then have sufficient time for the 'planned' activity. A programme like 'PEG' which has a competitive element, or a complex programme which has a number of different variables to manipulate, such as 'Slick' (British Petroleum, 1983) or 'Relationships' (BBC, 1984) can engage students for more than an hour; investigation of one section of 'Moving Molecules' could take ten minutes. Unlike a role-play it is possible to interrupt a computer program at any time simply by switching off the machine! Timing for using computer simulations is therefore no more difficult than for any other activity.

2. Classroom Management

Once students are seated and using computers classroom management is relatively easy. The main difficulty arises when large numbers of students require help simultaneously. 'Networking' of computers is one way of alleviating this particular problem. The provision of adequate instructions for use on screen is also helpful. Difficulties also arise where students have problems in reading instructions – this is where simple picture guidelines can be helpful.

3. Debriefing of Computer Simulations

The function of the debriefing is similar to that of other simulations; to evaluate the learning that has taken place. Sometimes no debriefing is necessary, for example, where 'Moving Molecules' is used as an integral part of the lesson, or as a demonstration. When the program has been used by students working more independently, then some discussion, ideally at the end of the lesson, would be essential. This debriefing can be very short as a lot of discussion normally takes place while students are using programs. Follow-up activities, such as questions which reinforce or extend the ideas explored in the program, can also be utilised.

The Role of Simulations in Science Education

Simulations, with the notable exception of computer simulations, are less frequently used in science than in other subject areas. There are many reasons why this should be so, including the practical nature of much science teaching. However, there are situations where first-hand experience is not possible or where it is important for students to explore ideas or feelings about controversial issues. It is in these situations, particularly those related to the understanding of of social, economic and environmental issues, or consideration of the history of science in a world context, that simulations can be employed as a very effective teaching strategy. These issues are now more widely recognised as being an important part of science education; they were an explicit element of the National Curriculum for Science in England and Wales (DES, 1989), particularly Attainment Target 17 – the Nature of Science – and still exist, though less obviously, in the 1991 version (DES, 1991). Examples of where simulations could be used include assessing the environmental impact of industrial waste, or the importance of genetic engineering for human populations, or the history of copper manufacture world wide. However, increased knowledge and understanding of complex issues, in the first example balancing the needs for industry with the need for conservation of habitats, is only one of the positive outcomes of using simulations. Other outcomes include those related to:

- the development of skills, particularly communication skills and social skills

- attitudes such as the ability to respect, and to listen to, other points of view, and increased motivation

- improved relationships, including those between students and between students and teachers and other adults

- the development of cross-curricular links

- making science more accessible to students with specific learning needs.

The outcomes may also include attainment in areas which may not be easy to quantify but which are of importance in personal development, for example, an increase in confidence in dealing with situations outside the school environment. Such situations include social interactions with peers and the ability to resist pressure, for example, to experiment with drugs.

Outcomes such as these are common to all types of simulations including very simple role-play activities. It is for these reasons, plus the increased knowledge and understanding of complex issues related to the nature and use of science, that simulations are a teaching strategy which merits consideration by science teachers.

References

Association for Science Education (1988) – *Science and Technology in Society*, Hatfield: Association for Science Education (ASE).
    Designed as extension material for teaching 14–16 year olds. The books include a number of simulation/role-play activities, e.g.
        502 – The Coal Mining Project
        503 – Paying for the National Health
        602 – The Limestone Inquiry
        608 – Should we buy a fall-out shelter?
        901 – The Chinese Cancer detectives
        1002 – Quintonal – an Industrial Hazard
    Some SATIS materials designed for discussion, such as 401: Fluoridation of Water Supplies, could be used to develop simulations.
Association for Science Education (1981) *'Dental Health Project' Science in Society Project*, Hatfield: Association for Science Education
    Role-play suitable for Y12 & 13 science and general studies groups; the more simple form described in this chapter was developed from SATIS unit 401 - 'Flouridation of Water Supplies'
British Gas (1983) *PEG – Primary Energy Game*, British Gas
British Petroleum (1983) *'Slick'* –
    computer game which involves predicting the path of an oil slick and then selecting the best method of dealing with the slick. It involves decision-making skills and practice in plotting coordinates.
British Broadcasting Corporation (1986) *Ecodisc*, BBC Enterprises in association with Acorn Computers.
    Interactive teaching material which allows study of different habitats; habitats can be 'managed' and outcomes simulated. The materials exploit the potential of linking video to a computer.
Brosnan, T. 'Using spreadsheets in the teaching of chemistry', *School Science Review*, Mar 1990, 71, p 256
Cade, A. (1986) *Pond Dipping Game*, Slough: Richmond Publishing Co
    Game which can be used in a variety of ways with groups from top primary to Y12 & 13 groups studying A-level biology. It is designed to help familiarise students with the organisms commonly found in ponds and to help them to gain an understanding of food chains and food webs.
Cambridge Educational Software (1983) *'Moving Molecules'*, Cambridge: Cambridge Educational Software
Computers in the Curriculum, *Relationships – Controlling Malaria in an African Village*, Science Topics – Computers in the Curriculum Project/British Broadcasting Corporation
ILEA (1989) *Modular Science Resources Book 1*, London: John Murray
    'Energy' card game designed for reinforcement and self-assessment. This book also contains details of a role-play suitable for 13–14-year-olds which is based on a public meeting called to debate the siting of a nuclear power station.
Lythe, M. and Gray, D. (eds) (1986) *Making Patterns 2*, London: Longman
        'Nitrogen Cycle Game', p.18 – see also
        'The Survival Game' in *Using Patterns*
        'The Random Walk Game' in *Making Patterns 1*.
Ogborn, J. (1990) 'A future for modelling in science education', *Journal of Computer Assisted Learning*, 6, pp. 103–12
Rogers, L. (1990) 'IT in the National Curriculum', *Journal of Computer Assisted Learning*, 6, pp. 246–54

Schools Council/Health Education Project (1982) *'Finding out about fluoride'*, Health Education 13–18, London: Forbes Publications

School Science Review, Journal of the Association for Science Education (ASE), Hatfield, Hertfordshire.

Further reading and resources

AVP (1992) *A Complete Guide to the Best Software for National Curriculum: Archimedes, BBC, IBMPC, RM Nimbus* (AVQ School Hill Centre, Chepstow, Gwent, NP6 5PH, UK)

Burdett, P. (1989) 'Adventures with N Rays: An Approach to Teaching about Scientific Theory and Theory Evaluation' in Millar, R. (ed.), *Doing Science: Images of Science in Science Education*, Lewes: Falmer Press

DES (1989) *Information Technology from 5–16, Curriculum Matters 15*, London: HMSO

Kahn, B. (1985) *The Use of Computers in Science Education*, Cambridge: Cambridge University Press

OXFAM – Poverty Game – can also involve participants in cooperative ventures and role-play

OXFAM – Chicken Game

Scarfe, J. and Wellington, J. (1993) *Information Technology in Science and Technology Education*, Buckingham: Open University Press

Stamp, R.D. and Harrison, W. (1975) *Science Games Part 1 and 2*, London: Longman
Package of games designed to be used as an adjunct to science courses; suitable for use by students of 10–16 years.

8
DISCUSSIONS

Arthur Jennings

While science in British schools has an international reputation for its emphasis on practical work, the place given to discussion has attracted little recognition. Indeed, many science teachers have paid little formal attention to the development of discussion in their lessons, though a certain amount of informal talk between two or three students working in a group on a practical task has long been regarded as acceptable. It has also been recognised that much of this conversation centres on the practical work in hand, though noise often grows to problematic levels. Positively to encourage talk as a deliberate learning activity requires confidence on the part of the teacher; confidence that the talk can be controlled and managed so that it is productive. However, in recent years several factors have combined to encourage teachers to provide more student discussion opportunities during science lessons. As teachers experiment with discussion techniques they are discovering that 'discussion' is a broad term that encompasses a range of learning activities, but which also requires an additional set of subtle teaching skills.

Curriculum influences

It may be helpful to identify some of the pressures which have elevated 'discussions' to an important component in science lessons, for in doing so several different applications of discussion techniques will become apparent. In the early 1970s the research and publications of the Writing Across the Curriculum Project (1975) drew attention to the importance of language in all subjects of the secondary curriculum. With modest publications such as *Writing in Science* and *From Talking to Writing,* the attention of science teachers was drawn to the function of the spoken and written word in learning science. The writings of Douglas Barnes (1976) and the Bullock Report (1975) added to these emerging insights. Science teachers began to appreciate that the language of science even at school level is highly specialised and an obstacle to learning for many children. This was an important message to teachers already aware of the work of Bernstein (1973) on social–class related differences in the way language is used to construct meaning. Meanwhile, in parts of the country, increasing numbers of science teachers were encountering students of ethnic minority groups for whom English is the language of school but not of home. Gradually science teachers developed a new consciousness with respect to their oral communication and began to examine the language of worksheets and textbooks with the purpose of making science more accessible. At the same time teachers accepted that the language barrier could only be bridged if students were expected to speak about science as well as reading and writing about it.

A quite different motivation was given to student talk by the Nuffield Science curriculum projects of the 1960s and 1970s. These projects adopted guided discovery as the principal teaching approach. In this context, discussion was seen as a vehicle by which students could generate hypotheses and then devise practical investigations to test their hypotheses. Further discussion followed to review experimental results and to generalise from them. Subsequently, further curriculum projects were developed which focused on the social impact of science. Projects such as Science and Society, SISCON in School and the SATIS Project feature the interactions of science and technology with the immediate everyday world in which students are growing up. These projects challenge young people to evaluate evidence, to make reasoned judgements and to express their ideas and convictions. Talk generated by these projects is far removed from the factual discourse of many didactic lessons, as has been well illustrated by the work of Solomon (1993).

In the 1980s the importance of talk in helping students to clarify, formulate and reformulate their scientific ideas became a major research focus. Followers of the 'constructivist' movement as articulated by the Children's Learning in Science Project will be aware of the importance attached to discussion (Scott, 1987). Teachers are recommended to allow students to express their ideas about scientific phenomena. Once this elicitation phase has been achieved teachers provide laboratory experiences which will confront any non-scientific ideas (alternative frameworks) which were exposed during the elicitation stage.

A most significant endorsement of the potential value of discussion in learning science was given by the Working Group commissioned to define the Attainment Targets and devise the Programmes of Study for Science in the National Curriculum. In their report, Science for Ages 5–16, they went so far as to suggest that there should be a profile component for Communication, which included an attainment target focused on students' ability 'to use a variety of communication skills in reporting, discussing and responding'. While this particular proposal did not survive in its original form in the statutory prescription, the substance remains. Communication skills feature prominently in the programmes of study. Thus at Key Stage 1, the programme of study reads:

> **Communication**: Throughout their study of science, students should develop and use communication skills and techniques involved in obtaining, presenting and responding to information. They should also have the opporunity to express their findings and ideas to other students and their teacher, orally and through drawings, charts, models, actions and writing. They should be encouraged to respond to their teacher and to the reports and ideas of other students and take part in group activities.

These sentiments are echoed with extensions at each of the succeeding Key Stages so that at Key Stage 4 students should be: 'encouraged to articulate their own ideas and work independently or contribute to group tasks'; and 'they should have opportunities to translate information from one form to another to suit audience and purpose'.

It is perhaps fair to conclude that National Curriculum Science embraces the old adage that 'every teacher is a teacher of English'.

Discussions — the potential

Given this background of development in educational thinking and curriculum change, the key message of this chapter is that discussion is an invaluable, multi-faceted tool for the teaching and learning of science. Discussions can be used so that thinking is stimulated, learning facilitated, scientific attitudes promoted and understanding of the nature of science nurtured. To achieve these desirable goals the teacher has to be clear about intended learning outcomes and to organise discussion opportunities in ways that will optimise the achievements of these goals.

Classroom climate

Before we examine more closely the particular skills and kinds of learning which discussions can enhance, it is necessary to consider the status of the learner in a discussion. The way a teacher uses language in the classroom carries implicit messages about the role of the student and about the teacher's view of science. If the teacher's language subtly suggests that there is a fixed body of knowledge which teacher possesses and which students need to accept and assimilate then students may feel that their ideas are scarcely worth expressing. Of course, students expect their teachers to be proficient in science. An invitation to students to speak about matters on which they can only guess at answers is likely to be treated with contempt. If we invite students to discuss we are seeking expression of their ideas, their views, their observations, conjectures and even, on occasions, their value judgements. But, having asked for their responses, we must ensure that these contributions are then taken seriously by both the teacher and other students. Immediately, this requirement spells out an essential quality for the classroom or laboratory climate in which effective discussions can take place. For certain kinds of discussion a laboratory with fixed benches may be far from ideal, but, as we saw in Chapter 2, a school science laboratory is a multi-purpose learning environment in which compromises and adaptability are essential. Much more important than physical layout is the inter-personal climate. Students will be inhibited if their teacher is authoritarian, sarcastic or dismissive but will be encouraged by a teacher who listens, shows interest and respects views expressed. Discussion will also be damaged if students are intolerant and make mock of new or different ideas. A necessary precursor for successful discussion is for the establishment of an atmosphere in which students and teacher work collaboratively and respectfully.

Listening to one another is a demanding skill and one that comes neither easily nor naturally to many adolescents. Humour is a further important ingredient of discussion. A teacher need not be alarmed by an occasional eruption into laughter. Sharing a joke can serve as a unifying factor within a group, but deliberate, calculated attempts to ridicule another student's viewpoint have no place in discussion directed towards cognitive learning. The hallmark of discussion as an educational activity is to learn from and with one another. Therefore, not only do teachers have to learn how to initiate, manage and capitalise on discussions but also students have to learn to discuss. This involves learning a complex pattern of unwritten rules. For this very reason students can only learn to discuss by engaging in discussion.

Flexible seating arrangements are ideal for discussion activities. While science laboratories usually have the obstacle of fixed benches, students' stools are mobile. Many teachers have learned to achieve flexibility for discussion work by forming small groups of two or three students along benches (see photographs in Chapters 3 and 4). These small groups may then be combined with groups from the next bench to groups of four or six. If required, these large groups can then be combined for a further stage of shared discussion. In the examples that follow, reference will be made to group organisation and reorganisation.

Small-scale discussions

Thus far we have seen that discussions are potentially powerful tools for students' learning but that they make considerable demands on both the teacher's skills and upon students themselves. Fortunately, discussion can be used flexibly. It is practicable and probably advisable to begin in a small way. Worthwhile discussion can occupy but a short part of a science lesson. Therefore teachers can feel their way and help their students to develop skills by using small group discussions involving students in groups of two or three for short interludes as components of the total lesson. The development and progression of an extended discussion will be considered later but first we shall examine a series of small group discussions of the kind that are easily incorporated into science lessons. As you enter in your imagination into each of these situations, pause to consider the kinds of thinking and the sorts of statements and questions which the students will be using.

Discussion 1

In groups of three, twelve-year-old students are examining a small, unfamiliar biological specimen, using magnifying glasses. The task is to decide whether it is an animal or plant and to compile a list of reasons to support a conclusion.

Discussion 2

A class of thirteen-year-old students has worked in small groups to perform a short, practical investigation. Each group has compiled a set of results and these results have been collated in table form with those from all the other groups. The class was then given further sets of results obtained from published scientific work and these results were accompanied by a summary of equipment used by scientists to obtain their results.

Each group of students has been asked to compare its results with:

    i. those of other groups in the class, and
    ii. the scientists' results.

Specifically, they have been asked whether the pattern of results is the same, to note differences between the results and, when differences occur, to suggest possible reasons.

Discussion 3

Students have been studying aspects of burning by using candles. A variety of candles has been used, including candles of different colour and shape, and it has been noted that not all candles burn at the same rate.

In small groups students have been given the task of planning an investigation to discover what properties of a candle affect the rate of burning. A secondary task is to list the materials necessary to conduct the investigation.

Discussion 4

After several lessons in which they have been studying human influence on the local environment, fourteen-year-old students have been divided into small groups to discuss three alternative by-pass routes for a proposed road around a country town. Students in each group have been supplied with a map showing the existing road network, population distribution, shopping and industrial areas and have further data relating to each possible route. This supplementary data includes geological, ecological and cost details for each route.

Students have been asked to work in their groups to select one route and to provide reasons for their decision, including amenity, social and economic factors as well as conservation of the local natural history and heritage.

Discussion 5

A group of four fifteen-year-olds has been set a design task. They have some knowledge of ecosystems and have recently been learning about adaptation to the environment and the 'survival of the fittest'. Now they have been given the specification of a small island, its geology, climate, flora and fauna. They have been asked to select a suitable ecological niche for which they are to design an animal which can survive without major distortion of the existing ecological balance. Their design is to include an outline of the life cycle to show how the creature will survive in its niche.

Discussion 6

Three A-level students are engaged in conversation in front of a computer screen. The programme models the production of sulphuric acid and their task is to optimise production with profitability. They may vary the pressure, temperature, the ratio of SO_2 and O_2 and whether or not to use a catalyst.

These discussion activities have involved students of different ages and while some of them are suitable for an early stage in a lesson, others are geared to the later stages after practical results have been obtained. Still others could occupy much of a lesson or be offered to some children who had already completed essential work. It will be apparent in every case that substantial preparation is needed by the teacher in readiness for the discussion. Materials and supporting documentation must be available and the task to be accomplished needs to be stated in precise terms. The amount of guidance necessary will depend on the age and experience of the learners and on the complexity of the task, but it should be noted that discussions are to be active. Students in all our examples were required to 'list', 'design', 'plan', 'select'. They were not simply invited to talk to one another as they felt inclined.

If you compiled a list as you read you probably noted that students engaged in these activities were required to recall knowledge, apply their knowledge, collect data and organise its presentation, search for patterns, select appropriate variables and critically evaluate as well as having opportunities for imaginative and creative thinking.

Management of discussion

The prerequisites for good discussion identified so far are a suitable interpersonal climate, well prepared supporting materials and precision in the purpose of the discussion task and what its outcome should be. However, this is only the beginning of the teacher's work. Presentation of the discussion specification is the next step. Skill is required to motivate students to engage in collaborative conversation. If this activity comes early in the lesson the teacher has to generate enthusiasm and to set the scene with enough detail to avoid confusion while not offering suggestions that may constrain the range of students' thinking. It is also vital to arrange a suitable seating arrangement quickly so that discussions can begin promptly without loss of interest and momentum. If the discussion task is to follow other class work the teacher's judgement is critical in deciding exactly when to stop the class and initiate the discussion.

Once discussion has started the teacher continues to have several duties to fulfil. Even though there may be several small groups conversing simultaneously the teacher has to try to monitor the discussions in several ways. It is important to tune in to individuals, to sample their ideas and detect their alternative frameworks. There will be occasions when the teacher will decide to intervene to provoke thinking, to challenge ideas students are expressing or to encourage participation from reticent students but the teacher needs to be restrained. It is important when the teacher joins in the discussion to do so more as an equal participant than as an authority seeking to correct ideas. Listening to groups enables the teacher to follow the trend of a group's ideas, to detect group dynamics and to identify issues from different groups worthy of further elaboration at class level. If small group work is a prelude to larger group or whole class discussion then the teacher has to judge when to move the groups along and how to rearrange the seating. It is also possible that an assessment dimension will be added to the teacher's role and this is considered later.

Extended discussion

An example of a lesson in which discussion is used as the major teaching strategy is elaborated below by following the course of a lesson which was based upon an observation exercise.

The teacher first carefully selected an object for observation. The object had to be unfamiliar to the students, sufficiently complex to present many features to be observed and available in quantity to allow all students to have a close-up view. At the start of the lesson the class was arranged in groups around the objects and for several minutes students were asked to observe. The students then worked individually to make a list of features they had observed. Meanwhile the teacher collected the objects and removed them from view.

In their groups of six to eight students, one person was then made recorder and in turn each student reported one observation from their written list. Opportunity was given for each student to contribute a second and even a third observation until a complete list of all the different observations had been compiled. The teacher had made it clear that all observations were to be recorded, even when one student's observation contradicted that of another. Furthermore, students were instructed to avoid argument and debate about reported observations during the stage of compiling the total list, even though some of the features reported as observations were really deductions made by the observer.

Once a group had completed its composite list the teacher returned the original object and the group was asked to work through its list and to agree which observations were accurate and which were mistaken. The second opportunity to look at the object was marked by keen interest and attention, not least because students were eager to check out their own contributions. By discussion, agreement was reached on a corrected set of observable features but not before the close attention to the specimen necessary to resolve differences had yielded additional features not noted at all on first observation. Discussion also highlighted those deductions which had been listed as observations, because students challenged one another about statements which went beyond what was visible and depended instead on prior knowledge or unwarranted assumption.

The teacher monitored progress in the groups towards an agreed list of observations and then decided to engage the class in a single discussion. After a quick seating reorganisation the teacher sought to change the level of discussion. Hitherto, talk had centred on reporting of observations, on considering the accuracy of interpretation and description. Now, by carefully chosen progressive questions, the teacher began to draw out differences between observations of one individual working alone and observations of a group working collaboratively. As students made their contributions the teacher listed points made on the overhead projector so that the class generated several conclusions, including:

- observations made by one person tend to be more limited in number and less reliable than those made by a group of people working together.
- an individual is more likely to jump to a conclusion when there are no others to provide a check.
- students differ in their ability to make accurate observations.

The teacher finally elected to take the discussion into a third phase by asking the class to consider objectivity in science. Students had now become aware of the unreliability of many of their observations. The terms 'subjectivity' and 'objectivity' were introduced and related to the notion of science as 'objective knowledge'. Students were encouraged to suggest ways in which science as an international activity can seek to maintain an acceptable degree of objectivity. Tentatively and in a non-specialised language students volunteered ideas about integrity in reporting, suspending judgement until there is sufficient evidence, the replication of experiments and re-working of results.

Notice how the teacher used discussion as a tool for learning. Students learned by first-hand experience that observations tend to be partial and selective. They were also introduced to the demands for scientific observation to be an active, searching activity with a deliberate caution against drawing premature conclusions. During the lesson the teacher sought to develop students' process skills and to nurture a better appreciation of the nature of science. Beginning with dual goals and with a planned strategy, the teacher had led the class through a carefully phased sequence. At every point the lesson was an active one for the students. They were required to observe, to record, to report, to check observations against the object, to evaluate different observations and then to reflect on differences between the effectiveness of individual efforts compared with those of a group. Finally, these experiences were related to science as a human activity. Throughout the lesson the teacher was also active. Setting the task and initiating observation depended on the teacher who then had to decide when to move activities on to the next phase. The teacher assumed a pivotal role as a kind of chairperson who introduced and led the second and third phases before undertaking the vital task of summing up.

Assessment

With respect to students' oral contributions and participation in discussion in science lessons, the national curriculum confers an assessment opportunity on teachers, in that it calls for much teacher assessment. It is not in any way being suggested that every word uttered by students is to be monitored and assessed, but it should be recognised that a shift in practice is intended. In the past assessment has concentrated on written and practical work, and with the exception of teacher observation of practical skills, practical achievement has often been assessed by the written outcome. Now there is encouragement to use a full repertoire of teacher assessment devices including oral assessment. Additionally for younger students and especially for some categories of special needs students the oral mode may assume prominence.

We have seen that discussions may be incorporated into science lessons which range over all four attainment targets. In this way teachers will be building up a picture of the students' achievements by a range of formal and informal assessments. Participation in group discussion involves a discrete range of discourse skills and teachers could beneficially evolve assessment techniques that are both valid and reliable. Inevitably a good deal of trial and error will be necessary to discover what can be assessed to an acceptable degree of reliability in the course of science lessons.

Group discussion: towards an assessment framework

With the intention of encouraging teachers to experiment in assessment of students while they are engaged in discussion work, especially for diagnostic purposes, a number of exploratory ideas are set out below. Furthermore, steps in this direction will do much to enable teachers to evaluate discussion activities in the learning process.

In the course of a group discussion a participant is expected to listen to others and to make some spoken contributions. In practice most participants make additional, non-verbal contributions. Thus, by gesture, laughter, eye and facial contact or body movement and posture, individuals may signal approval, interest and sympathy or indicate boredom and disapproval. These three dimensions of personal participation – speaking, listening and orientation towards group purpose – all deserve separate attention within an assessment framework.

i. Speaking

Assessment of a student's spoken contribution is the most accessible. The quantity and quality of a student's contributions can be monitored with the quality of statements being appraised against an hierarchical series such as:

> short statements of fact or opinion
> longer statements embracing several facts or ideas
> lengthy statements that embrace evidence and inference
> extended statements that deploy an argument, hypothesis or proposal.

ii. Group purpose

Observation of a group discussion will enable an assessor to identify those individuals who are helping a group to achieve its corporate task and those whose presence causes dysfunction. Monitoring facial expressions reveals the ebb and flow of mood and reaction. Thought will need to be given to achievement in group discussion for those students whose oral contribution is fairly minimal but whose support and encouragement to others help the group to generate a better level of discourse.

Group purpose may also be served by those students who do not lead but whose interventions challenge the group and may even set the group one stage further back, yet whose intention is positive in terms of rigour and integrity. By contrast, other speakers may appear fully supportive but towards a goal of a quick, even superficial completion of the group task, so that their effect is really subversive. Still other students may have a disruptive effect, not by intent, but because of a failure to hear what others have said or by misrepresentation of the words that were spoken.

iii. Listening

Assessment of listening skills presents a more difficult task, but this is an area worthy of exploration because of the potential for diagnosis of learning problems. Only by indirect evidence is it possible for a teacher to discern what a student is encoding as a result of what others in the group are saying. Attention by a student is essential in order really to hear what is said and clues about attentiveness may be picked up by observation. The factors discussed about group purpose relate to the quality of listening. Frequent contributions which ignore the flow of discussion and which recur in different groups and subject contexts may indicate a child in a special needs category, with a hearing defect, or an inability to encode a message from the words heard. Another student may lack the vocabulary to understand what is said while another may regularly select a single word or phrase to which to respond and whose speaking, therefore, misses the essential point. Still other students may hear the spoken messages correctly but owing to social maladjustment may not be able to respond positively. Therefore, while the teacher cannot 'hear' exactly what the student has 'heard', responses by the student which follow and develop the group discourse indicate appropriate reception. Frequent evidence of dysfunctional contributions to discussion suggest either a listening, receiving disability or a social maladjustment.

Talking and learning

At the start of this chapter it was observed that giving positive encouragement to students to talk requires confidence on the part of the teacher. To use discussions in the variety of ways and with the frequency that has been advocated also requires conviction on the part of the teacher that talking is important in learning. Traditionally teaching has been associated with transmission and learning with receiving. The National Curriculum report Science for Ages 5–16 placed its emphasis the other way round, for it speaks of students growing in competence in transmission and receiving. This emphasis implies an inversion of the traditional teacher/student talk ratio but, at the same time, it demands a higher level of activity by the student towards the end of acquiring knowledge and skills.

References

Barnes, D. (1976) *From Communication to Curriculum*, Harmondsworth: Penguin

Bernstein, B. (1973) *Class Codes and Control, Vol 1*, London: Routledge & Kegan Paul

Britton, J., Burgess, T., Martin, N., McLeod, A. and Rosen, H. (1975) *The Development of Writing Abilities, 11–18*, Schools Council Research Studies, Basingstoke: Macmillan Education

DES (1975) *A Language for Life (The Bullock Report)*, London: HMSO

Project team (1975) *Writing Across the Curriculum 11–13 Years*, Schools Council/Institute of Education

Medway, P. (1973) *From Talking to Writing ; Writing Across the Curriculum 11–13 years*, Schools Council/Institute of Education

Scott, P. with Dyson, T. & Gater, S. (1987) *Children's Learning in Science Project: A constructivist view of learning and teaching in science*, Centre for Studies in Science and Mathematics, The University of Leeds

Solomon, J. (1993) *Teaching Science Technology and Society*, Buckingham: Open University Press

Further reading

Association for Science Education (1988) *SATIS – Science and Technology in Society*, Hatfield: Association for Science Education (ASE).

Bentley, D. and Watts, M. (1992) *Communicating in School Science*, London: Falmer Press.

Sutton, C.(ed.) (1981) *Communicating in the Classroom*, Sevenoaks: Hodder and Stoughton

Sutton, C. (1993) *Words, Science and Learning*, Buckingham: Open University Press

APPENDIX
NATIONAL CURRICULUM

Jenny Frost

The national curriculum and assessment

The national curriculum, introduced into England and Wales in 1988, is still undergoing change (Dearing, 1993, SCAA, 1994); this account therefore gives only an outline of the position as it is at the time of writing.

The national curriculum is an 'entitlement curriculum' for all children during the eleven years of compulsory schooling, from age 5 to 16 years. These eleven years of schooling, labelled as 'years one to eleven' and written as Y1, Y2...11 are divided into four stages (referred to as 'Key Stages' and denoted by KS1–4). Years 1–3 form key stage one; years 4–6 form key stage 2; years 7–9 form key stage 3; and years 10 and 11 form key stage 4. If the changes recommended by Dearing are implemented the national curriculum will occupy 80% of the timetable for key stages 1, 2 and 3, and 60% of the timetable for key stage 4. These represent a reduction on the current percentages, and will allow schools greater flexibility and autonomy about how they implement and supplement the national curriculum.

The national curriculum is defined by subjects and cross-curricular elements. The subjects comprise:

> English, mathematics, science, Welsh (for schools in Wales where Welsh is the main medium of instruction), geography, history, art, music, technology, physical education, religious education, with a modern foreign language added at key stage 3.

If the Dearing report is implemented, geography, history, art and music will not be part of the compulsory curriculum for all students at key stage 4, although they will, of course, be included in the 'optional' curriculum for a large number of students.

The cross-curricular elements are described under 'dimensions, skills and themes'. They include such things as aspects of equal opportunities and education for life in a multicultural society; communication, numeracy, study, problem-solving, personal and social, and information technology skills; environmental education, education for citizenship, health education, careers education and guidance and economic and industrial understanding.

Assessment is a central feature of the national curriculum. Formative assessment is an intrinsic part of teaching, but at or near the end of key stages 1, 2 and 3, i.e. at ages 7, 11 and 14 years, teachers are expected to summarise their students' achievements on a ten-level scale (see below). The extent to which the teachers' assessments are supplemented by results from nationally devised tests and examinations is still a matter under discussion. Some means of standardisation of marking across schools is an essential feature of the scheme,

Attainment target 1	Attainment target 2	Attainment target 3	Attainment target 4
Scientific investigations	Life and living processes	Materials and their properties	Physical processes
(i) ask questions, predict and hypothesise	(i) life processes and the organisation of living things	(i) properties, classification and structure of material	(i) electricity and magnetism
(ii) observe, measure and manipulate variables	(ii) variation and the mechanisms of inheritance and evolution	(ii) explanation of the properties of materials	(ii) energy resources and energy transfer
(iii) interpret their results and evaluate scientific evidence	(iii) populations and human influences within ecosystems	(iii) chemical changes	(iii) forces and their effects
	(iv) energy flows and cycles of matter within ecosystems	(iv) the earth and its atmosphere	(iv) light and sound
			(v) the Earth's place in the Universe

Figure A 1. National Curriculum in Science: what is to be learnt is specified in terms of 4 attainment targets and 16 strands (DES, 1991)

Statements of attainment from strand on electricity	
level 1	know that many household appliances use electricity but that misuse is dangerous
level 2	know that magnets attract some materials and not others
level 3	know that a complete circuit is needed for electrical devices to work
level 4	be able to construct circuits containing a number of components in which switches are used to control electrical effects
level 5	know how switches, relays, variable resistors, sensors and logic gates can be used to solve simple problems
level 6	understand the qualitative relationship between current voltage and resistance
level 7	understand the magnetic effect of an electric current and its application in a range of common devices
level 8	be able to explain charge flow and energy transfer in a circuit
level 9	be able to use the quantitative relationships between charge, current, potential difference, resistance and electrical power
level 10	understand the principles of electromagnetic induction

Figure A 2. Examples of statements of attainment for 10 levels for Sc4, strand (i), Electricity and Magnetism (DES, 1991) whether done by the use of tests or other moderation procedures. Public examinations for GCSE (General Certificate of Secondary Education), will, for the time being, remain the assessment used at the end of key stage 4.

National curriculum science

Science was designated a 'core' subject along with mathematics, English (and Welsh), in 1988 and will remain so, even with the changes proposed. It is worth noting that before 1988, science was taught in only about 50% of primary schools and many students did not study science beyond the age of 14 (end of key stage 3). National curriculum science will undergo modification in the next two years, but many of its current features are likely to remain (SCAA, 1994).

Subjects in the national curriculum are sub-divided into what have been named 'attainment targets' (Science has four, denoted by Sc1–4, or ScAT1–4), and these are further subdivided into 'strands', of which there are 16 for science. Figure A1 shows the attainment targets and strands for science. Sc1, scientific investigations, involves students in learning how to undertake whole investigations, from initial generation of questions, through planning to interpreting data and evaluating experimental procedure. Investigation is a component of the science curriculum from year 1 to year 11. The attainment targets, Sc2–4, are concerned with knowledge and understanding of scientific concepts, facts and theories. Sc2 contains mostly the life sciences; Sc3 contains what traditionally might be thought of as chemistry and earth sciences; Sc4 contains physics and astronomy. Sc1 is intended to be taught in the context of Sc2–4.

This framework of attainment targets and strands is currently used in specifying:

- what is to be studied (programmes of study, PoS);
- what is to be learned (statements of attainment, SoAs).

Programmes of study are specified for each strand for each key stage, but not for each year. The following extract from the programme of study for key stage 3, attainment target 2, life and living processes, gives an indication of the level of detail which is given:

> Pupils should be introduced to pyramids of numbers and biomass as ways of quantifying relationships within food chains. They should study the cycling of materials in biological communities and be introduced to the classification of waste products of human activities as bio-degradable or non-biodegradable, and investigate ways of improving the local environment. (*National Curriculum Science*, HMSO, 1991, p.16)

Schools still have to plan and organise their own more detailed schemes of work. These do not, however, have to have the same structure as the national curriculum framework providing they incorporate the programmes of study and statements of attainment; consequently, integrated and co-ordinated science courses are possible.

Each science programme of study has an introduction concerned with the importance of: communication in science, understanding of social, economic and technological aspects of science and of the nature of scientific ideas. The introduction to KS4 programme of study begins:

> To communicate, to apply, to investigate and to use scientific and technological knowledge and ideas, are essential elements in the study of science. (*National Curriculum Science*, HMSO, 1991, p.22)

Attainment targets are also underpinned by 'statements of attainment' (SoA) which indicate what is to be learned at ten progressive levels for each strand. For science there are a total of 175 statements of attainment. An example of the SoAs for one strand, showing the 10 levels, is given in figure A2. The idea for the 10 level 'ladder' came from the original working party on assessment (DES, 1987); it is used to determine how far a child has progressed in a particular subject. For many subjects the statements of attainment have been used for trying to determine a child's 'level', while in other subjects, more global criteria have been used. 'Levels' are reported, as a rule, for a subject as a whole, so ways of combining assessments across strands have been developed.

There are no set text books, as there are in some other countries with a national curriculum; schools are free to choose resources as they wish. Teaching methods are not specified either. There is also no restriction on linking the teaching of science with the teaching of another subject to produce a more integrated scheme of work, but in practice little of this has been done at secondary level (KS3 and 4). Integration of subjects at the primary level (KS1 and 2) is more common.

References

Dearing, R. (1993) *Final Report on the National Curriculum and Assessment*, London: SCAA
DES (1991) *Science in the National Curriculum*, London: HMSO
Jennings, A. (1992) *National Curriculum Science: So Near and Yet So Far*, The London File, Institute of Education, University of London: Tufnell Press
NCC (1992) *Starting out with the National Curriculum*, York: National Curriculum Council
NCC (1993) *Teaching Science at Key Stages 1 & 2*, York: National Curriculum Council
NCC (1993) *Teaching Science at Key Stages 3 & 4*, York: National Curriculum Council
SCAA (1994) *Science in the National Curriculum*, London: HMSO
DFE (1995) *The National Curriculum*, London: HMSO

Note

1. As this book was going to press the revised national curriculum, which will come into force from August 1995 for KS3 and August 1996 for KS4, was published (DFE, 1995). The idea of levels is retained but with more general 'level descriptors' than the atomistic statements of attainment of the sort shown in figure A2. The content of Sc2–4 is reduced to a certain extent and there is less emphasis on whole investigations in Sc1. References above will provide the reader with more detailed outline accounts of the national curriculum and the national curriculum in science as they are now (NCC, 1992; NCC, 1993; DES, 1991), with background to NC science and its progress in the first few years (Jennings, 1992), and with the recent changes (Dearing, 1993; SCAA, 1994; DFE, 1995).

INDEX